SEVEN YEARS
of

Highly Defective People

Scott Adams' Guided Tour of the Evolution of **DILBERT**

BY SCOTT ADAMS

BOXTREE

First published in 1997 by Andrews and McMeel,
a Universal Press Syndicate Company, 4520 Main Street,
Kansas City, Missouri 64111, USA

This edition published in 1998 by Boxtree,
an imprint of Macmillan Publisher's Ltd,
25 Eccleston Place, London, SW1W 9NF
and Basingstoke

Associated companies throughout the world

ISBN 0 7522 2407 7

Copyright ©1997 United Feature Syndicate, Inc.

http:// www.unitedmedia.com/comics/dilbert

9 8 7 6 5 4 3 2 1

A CIP catalogue record for this book is available
from the British Library.

Printed and bound in Great Britain by
Butler & Tanner Ltd, Frome and London

Yeah, yeah it's for Pam.

Contents

Attention Mouse Potatoes!

Dilbert is never more than a click away!
Point your web browser to
www.unitedmedia.com and enter...

Everything you'd expect from a Dilbert web site:

- Comic strip that changes daily
- Time-wasting puzzles to get you through the work day
- Micromanagement tips to annoy your co-workers
- Free advice from Dogbert's Oracle

Plus, a glimpse into the secret past of Dilbert creator Scott Adams.

The Dilbert Zone is one of the top entertainment destinations on the World Wide Web. Praise for the Dilbert Zone has resounded from such lofty sources as the *Wall Street Journal* and *People* magazine.

Visit THE DILBERT ZONE today.
it's BETTER than WORKING

Introduction

You'll see a bunch of semi-legible, handwritten notes in the margins of this book. Those are mine. It's best to read each cartoon first and then the related note. Some of the notes are fascinating insights into the world of cartooning. Other notes are interesting only for their poor grammar and spelling, thus proving that you can be a moron and still have a successful career as a cartoonist. Either way, it's inspirational.

I made all of the notes in three sittings. I stopped only long enough to rest my weary hand. The thoughts are off the top of my head — which I can prove — because there's a little bald spot where the thoughts took off.

My hand is weary. That means the introduction is done.

Scott Adams

I was heavily into puns in the early days.

DILBERT

Dilbert was a doodle long before he had a name. He was a composite of my co-workers at Crocker Bank and later Pacific Bell. I worked with a lot of technical people and noticed that many of them had potato-shaped bodies and glasses. When I morphed them together in my brain they became Dilbert. I suppose I doodled the technical people more than other people because they seemed more interesting to me, both in personality and in appearance.

I'm often asked why Dilbert has no mouth and why his necktie curls up. The truth is that I don't know. The best answer I can give is that "it looks right." As a doodle, he was never drawn exactly the same. There were times in his doodle-days when he had a mouth and a flat tie. His body and head shape have changed gradually. He even had visible eyes once. In time I developed a preference for what "looked right" with him. It would be easy to interpret his lack of mouth and his uncontrolled necktie as symbols of his powerlessness, but I can't claim to be that clever. All I know is that I like him drawn that way.

I drew the little pre-Dilbert character to add interest to my own presentations at work. Sometimes I'd draw rebellious cartoons on the whiteboard of my cubicle for the amusement of my co-workers. People started wondering what his name was. It seemed appropriate to give him one. So I had a "Name the Nerd" contest on my whiteboard and invited people to write their suggestions below his picture.

Several people wrote in their suggestions, but none of them seemed right. Then a truly strange thing happened. My friend

9

Mike Goodwin stopped by to tell me he had the name. He picked up the erasable marker and wrote "Dilbert."

I ended the contest immediately and declared Mike the winner.

The strange thing is that there was a real sense of destiny about that moment. It didn't feel like Dilbert was being given a name, it felt like I was finding out what his name already was. I can't explain the feeling exactly, except that I knew it was important even then. It was a rare moment of complete clarity, when I knew I was in exactly the right place at the right time.

Much later, after Dilbert became syndicated, Mike realized how he had probably come up with the name. Mike's father had been a navy aviator during World War II and Mike still had some of his old navy documents and publications. In them were some cartoons that were well known to navy pilots of that period—cartoons about an incompetent pilot named Dilbert. The navy Dilbert, by a cartoonist named Osborn, appeared in single panel cartoons used to demonstrate what a pilot should never do by showing what happened when Dilbert did them all.

Had I known about the navy Dilbert cartoons I would have changed the name of mine, but it was too late by that point, happily. I'm glad to carry on the Dilbert tradition, albeit accidentally.

...at Home with Dogbert

HOO-HOO-HEE-HA!

...NO, THAT'S NOT IT.

DO YOU SUPPOSE OTHER PEOPLE PRACTICE LAUGHING WHEN THEY'RE ALONE?

OF COURSE.

TIME FOR YOUR SNEEZING DRILL.

OTHER PEOPLE MAKE IT LOOK SO NATURAL.

At first, Dogbert was the voice of Dilbert's insecurities.

WELL? WHAT DO YOU THINK OF MY NEW POEM?

I ONCE READ THAT GIVEN INFINITE TIME, A THOUSAND MONKEYS WITH TYPEWRITERS WOULD EVENTUALLY WRITE THE ENTIRE WORKS OF SHAKESPEARE.

BUT WHAT ABOUT MY POEM?

THREE MONKEYS, TEN MINUTES.

DO YOU LIKE MY NEW CLIP-ON NECKTIE?

IT'S VERY NICE. GOOD COLORS. NICE PATTERN. WHY, WITH A TIE LIKE THAT, DON'T BE SURPRISED IF YOU GET AN OFFER TO POSE FOR GQ MAGAZINE!

I THINK YOU CROSSED THAT FINE LINE BETWEEN POLITE LYING AND OUTRIGHT SARCASM.

THE MOMENTUM CARRIED ME.

Dogbert's legs were tiny in the beginning.

DILBERT®

By Scott Adams

HI. I'M FROM THE "ORGANIZATION FOR THE PROTECTION OF UGLY PEOPLE."

WE ARE DEDICATED TO ELIMINATING THE STEREOTYPE OF UGLY PEOPLE AS "SMART" AND "NICE."

OKAY, I'LL MAKE A DONATION.

1-21

THANKS, BUT THIS IS A MEMBERSHIP DRIVE...

I'M NEVER GOING TO ANSWER THE DOOR AGAIN.

DIDN'T HE RECOGNIZE YOU AS HIS GOD?

why are homely people discriminated against? we're the majority!

I shouldn't give away my secrets...to you weasels.

This joke was inspired by a friend who said his house "overlooked a mountain." It's the same pattern. How can you overlook a mountain? They're <u>huge</u>.

I have morning amnesia. I go through this whole routine every day.

13

So many people asked why Dilbert's tie points up that I decided to answer the mystery...

Then I realized I don't know why the tie points up myself. I left it a mystery.

I invented the word "nerdvana" based on my own computer bliss.

This was part of my early obsession with people who are bad at their jobs.

Dogbert allows me to have the conversations that happen in my head also happen in Dilbert's house.

I had a boss who always talked in dangerous, war metaphors. It seemed so out of place.

Dogbert is the perfect character to answer any ethical question.

why do beards stop at the neck?
I spend a lot of time wondering that.

ON MY FOURTH DAY OF TELECOMMUTING I REALIZE THAT CLOTHES ARE TOTALLY UNNECESSARY.

SUDDENLY I AM STRUCK BY A QUESTION: WHY DON'T MONKEYS GROW BEARDS?

HEY!

© 1995 United Feature Syndicate, Inc. (NYC)

2/9

I CALL A MEETING TO DISCUSS THE ISSUE BUT ATTENDANCE IS LOW.

ISSUE ONE: MONKEY BEARDS.

LET'S GO AROUND THE TABLE AND INTRODUCE OURSELVES.

. . . and Technology

MY NEW INVENTION SCREENS OUT ALL UNPLEASANT SIGHTS. TRY IT.

WELL, WHAT DO YOU THINK?

S. Adams

© 1989 United Feature Syndicate, Inc.

WHO SAID THAT?

THE HAND THAT USED TO FEED YOU.

4-21

Every invention has a non-obvious down side.

I THINK YOU SHOULD SEE A LAWYER BEFORE UNLEASHING THIS NEW INVENTION ON MANKIND.

LATER...

... I'M AFRAID MY NEW INVENTION WILL EXPOSE ME TO LOTS OF LAWSUITS.

© 1989 United Feature Syndicate, Inc.

S. Adams 5-5

WILL YOU ADVISE ME?

NO. SOUNDS LIKE I CAN MAKE MORE MONEY BY SUING YOU.

17

↰ Loosely based on my lawyer, who hasn't sued me yet.

Broccoli is a funny word. Watch this: "Hey, there's a weasel eating my broccoli!" HA HA HA! ... I kill me.

I was working in a high-tech research department when I wrote this. We would have been lucky to have that parsley invention.

18 This is an old joke that I cleverly modernized by adding the word "stealth."

For some reason, I find this line very funny. I don't know why.

I'm often asked what happens when I can't think of anything funny. The fin joke is a good example. What the hell was I thinking?

I had many performance reviews where it was not obvious what value I had created that year.

I prefer jokes where the visuals are in your head, so I don't have to draw **20** anything complicated. How do you draw a denture attack?

I think I have killed off more characters than any other cartoonist.

Have you ever wondered what makes something "news"?

I was sure my editor would put the boot on this cartoon, but she didn't.

I thought the android would become a regular, but he wasn't as interesting as I'd hoped.

Have you ever squinted to see if maybe you have X-ray vision. Admit it!

This is why I'm not a political cartoonist.

22

screwdrivers are the only tools I can draw.

Do I seem obsessed with hair?

I actually have an Intel video phone now. I'm waiting for someone **23** to call.

I had a calculator watch once. I replaced it with a watch that has a TV remote control built in (really

Techno-Bill is the most popular bit player I've ever introduced.

I'm an open-minded guy, but I do hate car salesmen. Does it show?

I think I know some people who own these suits already.

25

This happens to me — I have a great idea and then I make the mistake of telling someone else.

You might laugh at this invention, but I'm told that service people roll their clothes to prevent wrinkles when they pack. It could work! Try it at home.

A good name for a band would be "Tubular Luggage."

. . . in the Business World

I never know what to do in hallways. There's no graceful solution for shy people like me.

I saw someone do the carpet fuzz trick.

The best sickness excuse is, "You don't want to know the details."

27

My nose *always* itches when I speak in public.

In California, we fear people from New York City.

I worked with this secretary.

I did this cartoon after getting a complaint letter from a scientist.

29

I'm not smart enough to be a scientist, so I make my living by mocking them.

I'm amazed that this is legal in the USA.

A good metaphor can make any bad idea sound good.

DILBERT®

By Scott Adams

THIS CONCLUDES MY PROPOSAL TO THE EXECUTIVE COMMITTEE. ANY QUESTIONS?

NO, I THINK MOST OF US WERE THINKING ABOUT OTHER THINGS.

BUT HERE'S MY IMPRESSION OF WHAT YOU LOOKED LIKE GIVING THE PRESENTATION.

© 1991 United Feature Syndicate, Inc.

FUH FUH FUH FUH

NO, NO, IT WAS MORE LIKE...

FUH FUH FUH FUH

HOW DID YOUR PRESENTATION GO?

DON'T ASK.

S. Adams

FUH FUH DON'T ASK FUH FUH FUH FUH...

4-21

This cartoon is based on the most evil executive I ever met. He actually mocked people this way.

31

I should have put "velcro" in quotes because it's a trademark. oops.

When I ate lunch with the engineers at Pacific Bell, the one-upping continued until the food was all gone.

The more I exaggerate a character, the more he's familiar. It's strange.

Yes, I did get complaints from the vertically challenged.

This is perhaps the weirdest character I've ever created. He's based on a particular co-worker I once had.

I've known people who could sleep during meetings with no sense **33** of shame. I envy them.

Sleeping at work is a common theme in Dilbert. I used to sleep in my cubicle all the time.

I was raised in the country, where touching means you're standing on the same carpet. Any closer and you're engaged.

Empowerment might be the all-time dumbest idea, at least when it's over-applied.

34

DILBERT, I'M PUTTING YOU ON A ROTATIONAL ASSIGNMENT...

YOU WILL BE WORKING IN MARKETING UNTIL FURTHER NOTICE.

4-6

MARKETING
TWO DRINK MINIMUM

© 1992 United Feature Syndicate, Inc.

When I worked in Engineering, the marketing department was our evil nemesis.

DILBERT IS TRANSFERRED TO MARKETING

YOU LOOK LOST.

I NEVER KNEW THAT MARKETING WAS LIKE THIS ... DO YOU PEOPLE DO ANY WORK?

4-7

WELL, NOT ON "BARBECUE TUESDAY." ARE YOU STAYING FOR LUNCH? IT'S UNICORN!

© 1992 United Feature Syndicate, Inc.

It always seemed like Marketing had all of the party people.

DILBERT IS TRANSFERRED TO MARKETING

EVERY TUESDAY WE BARBECUE A UNICORN.

MAKE MINE RARE. HA HA! GET IT? RARE?

© 1992 United Feature Syndicate, Inc.

I'M NOT SURE I BELIEVE THIS IS THE "BEST PART."

4-8

I got complaints from unicorn lovers.

35

This joke was written by a reader as part of a fill-in-the-punchline contest. So don't blame me.

Some of my Pacific Bell co-workers longed for jobs where they would never be noticed.

36

I'm 5'8" and it bugs me when big oafs don't look where they're going.

...SO THEN I SPENT A YEAR IN EUROPE AND BLAH BLAH BLAH BLAH.

HEY, I THINK I CAN SEE YOUR BRAIN THROUGH YOUR NOSE!

ANYWAY... YOU WERE SAYING..?

I always say the wrong thing, usually because I'm bored.

IT LOOKS LIKE BRENDA HAS BEEN BRAINWASHED BY THE NEW COMPANY SLOGAN.

QUALITY... QUALITY...

IT ALL STARTED WHEN WE GOT THESE LITTLE STICKY NOTE PADS THAT SAY "QUALITY" ON THEM.

OOPS, SORRY, I SHOULDN'T PUT IT RIGHT IN YOUR FACE...

QUALITY... QUALITY... QUALITY...

I was part of a "Quality" initiative where the only tangible change was to our notepads.

GEE, TIM, YOU LOOK AWFUL.

I'VE BEEN WORKING FOR FIVE DAYS WITHOUT ANY SLEEP TO FINISH THIS REPORT.

AT FIRST I HAD A MENTAL BLOCK. BUT ON THE FOURTH DAY I WAS VISITED BY AN INCAN MONKEY GOD WHO TOLD ME WHAT TO WRITE.

WOW, LUCKY BREAK.

NOW I JUST HAVE TO FIND SOMEBODY WHO CAN TRANSLATE HIS SIMPLE BUT BEAUTIFUL LANGUAGE.

I had a co-worker who didn't realize how much the quality of her output was influenced by sleep deprivation.

I have to say "Camp Girl" instead of using a real organization's name. We fear them.

I spent most of my career in corporate America suffering from door envy.

I relished the small revenges.

This was inspired by my own tragic experiences at "team building."

AT THE "RIVERS AND TREES" MANAGEMENT COURSE.

THIS NEXT EXERCISE IS ALWAYS A FAVORITE.

USING ONLY A ROPE, YOUR TEAM MUST FIGURE OUT HOW TO CROSS THE MUDDY PATCH WITHOUT GETTING YOUR FEET DIRTY.

I COULD HAVE BEEN A FOREST RANGER, BUT NO-O-O-O...

It's hard to draw mud!

WHAT HAPPENED TO YOU?

I ASKED FLOYD A QUESTION.

FLOYD HATES HIS JOB, SO HE TAKES IT OUT ON CO-WORKERS. HE ALMOST CHEWED MY CLOTHES OFF.

HOW'D YOU STOP HIM?

HE WENT INTO SYNTHETIC SHOCK; IT'S NOT HEALTHY TO EAT TOO MUCH OF THIS STUFF.

I favor the death penalty for any co-worker who intentionally causes discomfort.

WHAT?! YOU THINK I'LL HELP YOU JUST BECAUSE I'M YOUR CO-WORKER?? HA! I HATE CO-WORKERS!

ALL I NEED IS...

I HATE THIS JOB! I HATE EVERYTHING! THE ONLY THING I LIKE IS BEING MEAN TO CO-WORKERS WHO NEED THE VITAL INFORMATION THAT I CONTROL!

IF YOU THINK YOU HATE HIM, YOU SHOULD TRY BEING HIS SECRETARY.

In every job, there was always one of these guys.

40

It's a common fantasy to bump off an obnoxious co-worker. (or is it just me?)

This is why I don't work in sales.

DILBERT®

BY SCOTT ADAMS

DILBERT, I WANT YOU TO INTERVIEW THE JOB APPLICANT WHO'S COMING IN TODAY.

SEE IF HE'S GOT WHAT IT TAKES TO BE AN ENGINEER.

HI, KARL. WE'LL START WITH THE STANDARD ENGINEERING TEST.

OKEY-DOKEY.

I HAVE THIRTY-FIVE PENS AND PENCILS HERE. HOW MANY ARE REALLY NEEDED TO PERFORM YOUR JOB?

ALL OF THEM.

CORRECT... NOW, WHAT IS THE PROPER WAY TO CARRY THEM WITH YOU?

RIGHT AGAIN. LAST QUESTION: WHAT IS THE ADVANTAGE OF WEARING NATURAL FABRICS?

UH-OH... PANIC SITUATION.

I... I DON'T KNOW.

THAT'S OKAY. I WAS TESTING YOUR HAIR. YOU'RE AN ENGINEER.

I used to quiz engineers about why they carry so many writing tools at once. As far as I can tell, it's so they'll have emergency backups.

42

DILBERT HAS AGREED TO TALK TO THE CLASS ABOUT EXCITING CAREERS IN THE FIELD OF ENGINEERING!

THERE'S MORE TO BEING AN ENGINEER THAN JUST WRITING TECHNICAL MEMOS THAT NOBODY READS.

4-20

ONCE IN A WHILE, SOMEBODY READS ONE. THEN YOU HAVE TO FIND A SCAPEGOAT, OR USE SOME VACATION TIME AND HOPE IT ALL BLOWS OVER.

© 1993 United Feature Syndicate, Inc.

I never knew what an engineer did for a living when I was a kid. I still don't.

DILBERT TALKS TO A CLASS ABOUT CAREER OPTIONS.

ENGINEERING IS ONE OF THE BEST CAREERS AVAILABLE.

FOR THE NEXT TWENTY YEARS I'LL SIT IN A BIG BOX CALLED A CUBICLE. IT'S LIKE A RESTROOM STALL BUT WITH LOWER WALLS.

4-21

I SPEND MOST OF MY TIME HOPING THE ELECTROMAGNETIC FIELDS FROM MY OFFICE EQUIPMENT AREN'T KILLING ME.

© 1993 United Feature Syndicate, Inc.

It's a good thing that nobody tells kids what work is really like.

DILBERT TALKS TO A CLASS ABOUT CAREER OPTIONS.

THE GOAL OF EVERY ENGINEER IS TO RETIRE WITHOUT GETTING BLAMED FOR A MAJOR CATASTROPHE.

4-23

ENGINEERS PREFER TO WORK AS "CONSULTANTS" ON PROJECT TEAMS. THAT WAY THERE'S NO REAL WORK, BLAME IS SPREAD ACROSS THE GROUP, AND YOU CAN CRUSH ANY IDEA FROM MARKETING!

© 1993 United Feature Syndicate, Inc.

...AND SOMETIMES YOU GET FREE DONUTS JUST FOR SHOWING UP!

GET OUT OF MY CLASSROOM.

 This is more truth than exaggeration.

The guy in the cubicle across the hall from me coined the phrase "sensory deprivation chamber" for his cubicle. I liked it.

You say bologna, I say baloney.

45

I like the phrase "germ-riddled children."

Yes, I *know* there's no such thing as the Vulcan death grip, even on "Star Trek."

Every company is better than your own. It's a rule of the universe.

↖ Note the elaborate use of background.

There's a reason that executives lie. The alternative is worse!

DILBERT THE MENTOR

THIS IS YOUR COMPUTER.

WHEN YOU HEAR FOOTSTEPS IT'S A GOOD IDEA TO MOVE THIS THING AROUND AND CLICK IT.

THIS CONCLUDES YOUR TECHNICAL TRAINING. IF YOU HAVE FURTHER QUESTIONS JUST REMEMBER YOU'RE INCONVENIENCING ME.

when people are mentored, they do in fact hold their arms out like that.

I HEAR YOUR COMPANY IS TRIMMING TRAVEL BUDGETS.

CAN ANYONE LEND ME BUS FARE TO GET HOME?

This is a rare action-oriented strip. I don't do many because they take longer.

I... I'D LIKE PERMISSION TO KEEP A PLASTIC PLANT IN MY CUBICLE.

CUBICLE GESTAPO

PERMISSION DENIED! PLANTS ATTRACT BUGS. IF I CAN'T TELL IT'S PLASTIC HOW ARE THE BUGS GOING TO KNOW THE DIFFERENCE?

WITH ALL DUE RESPECT, BUGS ARE WAY SMARTER THAN YOU.

OH YEAH? I'D LIKE TO SEE THEM DO THIS JOB.

when this appeared in papers, we changed "Gestapo" **48** to "police" to avoid complaints.

My publisher adds the color to these. They pick the worst possible times to add diversity to the cast.

HAVE A NICE NIGHT, DILBERT.

YOU CAN REST EASY KNOWING I'LL BE GUARDING THE BUILDING ALL NIGHT.

TO A CRIMINAL, THIS PLACE MUST LOOK LIKE A BIG OL' SHOPPING MALL.

THE CUBICLES ARE LIKE LITTLE STORES, EACH WITH ITS OWN SELECTION OF QUALITY MERCHANDISE.

IF YOU KNEW WHERE TO LOOK, YOU COULD GET PICTURE FRAMES, POSTAGE STAMPS, CLOCKS, AND EVEN FOOTWEAR.

ODDLY ENOUGH, YOU AND THE JANITOR ARE THE ONLY ONES HERE AT NIGHT, AND YET MY SNACK DRAWER KEEPS GETTING EMPTIED.

10-24

IT'S TOTALLY INEXPLICABLE.

WELL, GOOD NIGHT.

SHALL WE HEAD OVER TO "CHEZ DILBERT"?

LATER... THERE'S A SALE AT "WALLY'S SHOE WORLD."

We used "police" instead of "Gestapo" for newspapers on this one too.

By this time I was having serious hand problems, so the lettering was being inked by another artist. My hand got much better, but I continued this method to save time

Casual clothes are a double-edged sword.

I REALIZE THAT CASUAL DRESS DAY ISN'T EASY FOR YOU ENGINEERS...

BUT YOU'VE EXCEEDED THE BOUNDS OF GOOD TASTE. I'VE GOT TO SEND YOU HOME TO CHANGE.

SHUT UP, WALLY.

I HEARD THEY WERE BACK! I SWEAR!

I get more requests for casual day jokes than for any other topic.

ACCORDING TO YOU, IF I CUT YOUR BUDGET THE WORLD WILL ABRUPTLY STOP SPINNING AND WE'LL BE FLUNG INTO SPACE.

WHEREAS, THE RISK OF CUTTING DILBERT'S PROJECT IS "...A PLAGUE OF LOCUSTS O'ER THE LAND."

I'LL CUT BOTH PROJECTS. WITH ANY LUCK, WE'LL FLING THE LOCUSTS INTO SPACE.

LOCUSTS. REAL GOOD.

I was never good at protecting my budget because I was a terrible liar.

SOMETIMES I THINK THESE CONSTANT REORGANIZATIONS ARE JUST EXCUSES FOR GETTING RID OF UNWANTED EMPLOYEES.

WHAT JOB DID YOU END UP WITH?

ORGAN DONOR.

MY SHOULDER IS ACTING UP. DO I TALK TO YOU OR IS THERE A FORM TO FILL OUT?

I DON'T THINK THAT'S AN "ORGAN."

↰ You know it's true!

The pager-in-the-toilet problem is real. I've heard lots of stories about it.

OUR DEVICE CONFORMS TO ALL INTERNATIONAL STANDARDS FOR COMMUNICATIONS.

IN OTHER WORDS, IT DOESN'T DO ANYTHING USEFUL AND IT'S NOT YOUR FAULT.

IS THERE SOMEBODY LESS EXPERIENCED I COULD TALK TO?

DO YOU HAVE MY BOSS'S NUMBER?

I never draw these side view mouths anymore.→ 🔲 Now I do these →

THP-P-P-P-P

I CAN'T HEAR YOU! LA-LA-LA-LA-HM-HM-LA-LA

HE'S RIGHT! IT IS JUST LIKE A LITTLE FORT!!

FRIDAY MEETINGS.

I've never accomplished anything during a Friday meeting (except getting comic fodder).

WE COULD HAVE OUR NEXT ALL-DAY STAFF MEETING AT MY HOUSE.

DO YOU HAVE ACTUAL FURNITURE?

SOMEBODY WILL HAVE TO SIT IN THE BATH-ROOM.

I CALL BATHROOM

Everywhere I've lived, visitors look at my home 53 and say, "Did you just move in?"

Wally looks so cute in a jacket.

I had a project with a big budget once. It was like "Night of the Living Dead" as the zombies surrounded me.

Dilbert is the kind of guy who makes the best of a situation.

I believe cubicles were invented by someone who didn't like people.

when engineers eat bananas, it destroys their credibility.

As a rule, anything in a binder has very little value, except as building material.

↰ This happened to me often.

This exact thing happened to me, not counting the attractive outfit.

57

I experimented with doing my lettering by computer. In the end it was easier to have a human do it. Readers complained about the regularity of this lettering.

The urge goes away in the fifth year, typically. Never work in the same place for five years.

Every group has a pathological liar.

WE'RE ANNOUNCING TWO NEW PROGRAMS FOR EMPLOYEES.

THE FIRST IS A NEW DIGNITY ENHANCEMENT PROGRAM AND THE SECOND IS OUR NEW RANDOM DRUG TESTING INITIATIVE.

THE CLUE METER IS READING ZERO.

YOU EACH GET A HANDSOME COFFEE MUG AS PART OF THE KICK-OFF.

Motorola employees suggested this plot, which is loosely based on their company.

DROP YOUR TROUSERS AND TURN AROUND. I NEED A DNA SAMPLE.

WE'RE SCANNING FOR ANY FATAL GENETIC PROBLEMS THAT COULD HURT PRODUCTIVITY.

UH... WE DECIDED TO MOVE YOUR PROJECT DEADLINE UP A WEEK.

This day will come.

WE NEED TO FINISH YOUR PROGRAM TWICE AS FAST, SO I'M ADDING A PERSON TO HELP YOU.

YOU MIGHT NEED TO TRAIN HIM A LITTLE BEFORE HE'S PRODUCTIVE.

WARNING! WARNING! DR. SMITH

TELL ME AGAIN WHAT THE BIG GLOWING THING IS.

should have been ↑ "Mr." Smith, a
reference to the
old "Lost in Space" TV show.

DILBERT®

BY **SCOTT ADAMS**

LET ME INTRODUCE YOU TO ONE OF OUR ENGINEERS.

KAREN IS OUR NEW VICE PRESIDENT. AND YOU ARE...?

DILBERT: VALUED EMPLOYEE.

I BELIEVE IN OPEN COMMUNICATIONS, DILBERT. FEEL FREE TO TALK ABOUT ANYTHING.

UH-OH

SO, WHAT WERE YOU WORKING ON?

OH-NO

WELL... I WAS JUST SENDING AN E-MAIL TO SOMEBODY WHO SITS BY A WINDOW TO ASK IF IT'S RAINING.

IF IT'S RAINING I'LL FASHION A RAINCOAT FROM A LARGE TRASH BAG.

WATCH.

THREE HOLES AND YOU'RE READY TO GO!

ARE YOU PLANNING TO GO OUT AT LUNCH?

ONLY IF IT RAINS.

Garbage bags are often used this way in the seattle area.
They call it an "Engineer's Raincoat!"

60

At Digital Equipment Corporation they call this process "Densification."

cubicles are better than maximum-security prisons, but about the same as minimum-security, I'll bet.

I like to put opposites together. I've heard stories about motivational speakers who depress people.

WHO NEEDS TO SIGN MY BUSINESS CASE TO BUY A WEB SERVER?

HMM...THIS CROSSES ALL DEPARTMENTS. I FEAR IT. GET THE APPROVAL OF EVERY DIRECTOR, EVERY VP, EVERY EVP, PLUS GRIFFIN.

DO YOU MEAN TED GRIFFIN IN FINANCE OR THE MYTHICAL GRIFFIN BEAST THAT'S HALF EAGLE, HALF LION?

WHICHEVER IS HARDER.

I heard from lots of people named Griffin.

... and Women

I CAN REMEMBER WHEN THESE WERE ONLY FIFTEEN CENTS.

BUT I'M REALLY DATING MYSELF NOW...

WELL, IT'S NOT AS IF ANYBODY ELSE WOULD DATE YOU.

This is the very first Dilbert strip published. The setup line is something I heard from a lonely engineer. The punchline I kept to myself.

THERE... MY PROGRAM PROVES THAT PRETTY WOMEN HAVE EXTREMELY BAD PERSONALITIES.

THIS IS BASED ON THE INPUT THAT PRETTY WOMEN ARE NEVER NICE TO ME.

WHY DOES THE SCREEN SAY, "OR YOU ARE A GEEK"?

DARN! I THOUGHT I FIXED THAT BUG.

This was based on my personal experience.

I was just starting as a cartoonist and hadn't decided how to draw women's faces at this point.

Anything with the words "Dingo dog" is funny.

I had some blind dates in my dating days.
I would have been happy with this outcome.

If men were perceptive,
they'd never get lucky.

I've actually stopped breathing in elevators because I think it sounds loud.

I took a lot of heat for this cartoon. I meant it to be about a woman who was gigantic in general, but it comes off as a fat joke.

Do frogs have noses? They're hard to draw.

This sounds naughtier than it is.

Talking dogs are funny.

what do you do at the end of a bad date?

The original text said "virgin" not "maiden." It was softened so it wouldn't draw complaints in conservative towns.

Nice lips, eh?

It's a good thing women have no idea
what men think.

My first girlfriend used
to use this excuse.

68

69 A lot of readers didn't get this one. Hint: which = witch.

. . . and His Ego

I imagine an ego looks like this. It's a cross between a brain and a cloud.

My obsession with hair loss continues.

This is the sort of cartoon I draw when I'm not getting enough sleep.

I couldn't figure out how to end this sequence...

... It just kept getting stranger.

There!

I ended this one quickly.

. . . Dies

I killed Dilbert because sales to newspapers were slow. I thought this would shake things up. I don't think anyone noticed.

I want to be stuffed when I die.

YIKES! DILBERT'S INVENTION IS ALIVE!!

FLASH!

I AM A HOLOGRAPHIC RECORDING OF THE LATE DILBERT, WITH A MESSAGE TO DOGBERT FROM BEYOND THE GRAVE.

...AND MY RECIPE FOR CHILE CON CARNE IS AS FOLLOWS...

← He's so cute with his ears up.

UGH...GOSH, WHAT A NIGHTMARE.

BOB, I JUST DREAMED DILBERT WAS KILLED BY DEER, AND ALL HE LEFT ME WAS HIS RECIPE FOR CHILE CON CARNE.

BAD NEWS...

HE'S REALLY DEAD?

AND HIS CHILE CON CARNE STINKS.

My bid for reader sympathy failed. I decided to bring Dilbert back.

PLEASE, MISTER GARBAGE MAN, HELP US FIX DILBERT'S CLONING DEVICE AND BRING HIM BACK TO LIFE!!

THIS SHOULDN'T BE TOO HARD... STANDARD ANTI-LIGHT RESONANCE FILTERS... YEAH, I THINK I HAVE PARTS IN THE TRUCK.

YOU'RE GOING TO CLONE HIM FROM HIS OWN GARBAGE?

DON'T TELL ANYBODY-- THERE MIGHT BE A STIGMA.

© 1990 United Feature Syndicate, Inc.

S. Adams

Is anti-light the same as dark?

I was tired of this series, but it needed a conclusion.

. . . Travels

It seems as if I always get the worst seat.

I got complaints from people who don't think cannibal jokes are funny.

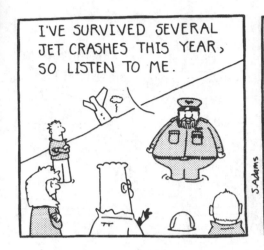

I'VE SURVIVED SEVERAL JET CRASHES THIS YEAR, SO LISTEN TO ME.

THE BEST WAY TO PREVENT FROSTBITE IS TO RUB WORCESTERSHIRE SAUCE ON YOUR BODY AND WHACK YOURSELF REPEATEDLY WITH A MEAT TENDERIZER.

I WONDER WHY HE HAD ENOUGH OF THESE FOR EVERYBODY?

WHACK WHACK

. . . Attempts to Join the Consumer Society

WELCOME TO ELECTRODE HUT. I'M HALF YOUR AGE, AND I KNOW MORE ABOUT ELECTRONICS THAN YOU EVER WILL. MAY I HELP YOU?

YES. I WOULD LIKE A HALF-DOZEN NIAD PULSE CONVERTERS AND AN ANZA BRUSH.

OR AM I BLUFFING?

THIS GUY IS GOOD.

In case you wondered, there's no such things as NIAD Pulse converters or ANZA Brushes.

I'M LOOKING FOR A FINE WOOL SUIT, IN THE $700 RANGE. SOMETHING FASHIONABLE YET TIMELESS.

TRY THIS $35 NYLON BEAUTY, SUITABLE FOR SWIMMING OR DINING OUT. THE BELL BOTTOMS ARE NO EXTRA CHARGE.

WOW!

I GUESS I WAS JUST BORN TO BE A FASHION PIONEER.

My pet peeve is that Salespeople always steer me to the cheapest items.

My first job was as a bank teller.

I love tods, even though I don't use them.

Women don't understand.

When I was a bank teller, I was robbed twice at gunpoint. I fantasized about beating up customers.

I'm a shy shopper. I don't like to be a burden to the salespeople so I always say, "Just looking."

If this existed, someone would buy it.

It's funny to me that I have to prove to the bank that I'm honest.

When I was a kid, my grandmother convinced me that brown eggs were tastier. Now I just wonder what route they took through the hen.

This might actually work someday.

CAN YOU HELP ME?

NO, I'M AFRAID I CAN'T.

YOU SEE, I GET PAID THE SAME LOW HOURLY WAGE WHETHER YOU BUY THAT SHIRT OR NOT. AND AFTER YEARS IN THIS BUSINESS I'VE LEARNED TO DESPISE THE GENERAL PUBLIC.

PLEASE... I HAVE EXACT CHANGE.

I HAVE NO WAY OF KNOWING IF THAT'S TRUE

I believe all salespeople hate me. If they didn't before, they do now.

I'M GOING TO THE BIG TECHNOLOGY SHOW.

WHAT DO YOU DO THERE?

I WILL WADE THROUGH A VAST SEA OF MOSTLY CURLY-HAIRED GUYS WITH FACIAL HAIR AND GLASSES. AND I WILL LOOK AT THOUSANDS OF INDISTINCT PRODUCTS.

IT'S LIKE SALMON RETURNING TO ITS BIRTHPLACE.

BUT WITHOUT THE SPAWNING OPPORTUNITIES.

Why do so many technology people have curly hair and glasses?

AT THE TRADE SHOW...

UH-OH. A VENDOR IS SCANNING ME.

I'M CAUGHT IN A TRACTOR BEAM! RED ALERT! RED ALERT!

LOSING LIFE SUPPORT SYSTEMS... ZZZZ

... AND IT CAN EVEN CALCULATE FRACTIONS!

All vendor demos are boring. It's the law, I think.

I support equal rights for pets.

In the beginning, Dogbert still had traces of dog-like behavior.

My cat does this.

DOGBERT

My personal experience with dogs was primarily with a beagle named Lucy, our family dog for most of my childhood. Lucy never once came when I called—not once in fourteen years. In fact, she did absolutely nothing except what she wanted to do. If I tried to pet her she would growl, grab my shirt by the cuff, rip the entire sleeve off, and run down the hall with it like a trophy. (That actually happened.) It was quite obvious that my family was subservient to the dog. Lucy slept on any furniture she wanted, she came and went as she pleased, never wore a leash, and had food and water served at her discretion.

Dogbert took on a bit of Lucy, particularly the beagle ears, round body, and attitude. He also took on a bit of the dark side of my own personality, the part that wants to conquer the planet and make all the people my personal servants.

Dogbert gets to say all the things that I might be thinking but can't say for fear of retribution. His view is that the entire world and all the people in it are here for his personal entertainment.

There's no explanation of why Dogbert chooses to live with Dilbert, except that he finds him amusing. Once in a great while we'll see some glimpses of affection. And if Dilbert gets in deep trouble we can count on Dogbert to bail him out.

Dogbert was more of a pet in the first year. He wasn't obedient, but he was a pet.

Dogbert is starting to show his true personality now.

I don't remember why I thought Dogbert should be egg-shaped.

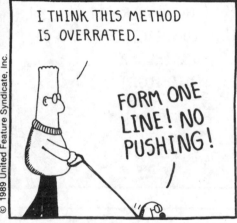

I can't imagine putting Dogbert in a leash now.

Dogbert shows emotion with fur, eyebrows, and ears.

This is my view of "roughing it," as expressed by Dogbert.

Here I was still playing with dog stereotypes. No dogs complained.

He's too cute when his ears fly up.

Dogbert begins to get political. Or maybe it was just an excuse to show what dogs look like with hats.

Have you ever noticed how many wealthy industrialists started out by doing illegal things? I'd love to see some statistics on that. And more dogs with hats.

Personally, I <u>love</u> capitalism, but it's a great subject for humor because it creates losers more often than winners. (I've been both.)

THIS IS SO NICE... JUST A MAN AND HIS MUTT OUT FOR A WALK.

"MUTT"?!

I THINK OF IT MORE AS A "CANINE AND A CLOD" OR A "DOG AND A DUMMY"... MAYBE A "POOCH AND A PINHEAD" OR A "BOWSER AND A BLOCKHEAD."

I THINK THAT'S ENOUGH.

A "HOUND AND A HINEY."

If a human had spoken the word "hiney," I probably wouldn't have gotten away with it.

DOGBERT, I HAVE COME FOR YOU.

YOW!

WAIT WAIT! DON'T I GET TO CHALLENGE YOU TO SOME CONTEST TO PLAY FOR MY LIFE!!?

OKAY... I THROW THIS FRISBEE — YOU TRY TO CATCH IT IN YOUR MOUTH.

DID YOU HAVE ANYTHING MORE DE- GRADING?

I always feel sorry for dogs who catch "Frisbees." It looks humiliating.

FREEZE!!! I'M A DOG CATCHER!

WHAT, NO COLLAR? YOU'RE GOING TO THE PUPPY PENI- TENTIARY, PAL!

YOUR HUMAN TURNED YOU IN?

HE DIDN'T THINK A PIT BULL SHOULD WEAR HIS HAIR THIS WAY.

This might be the world's first gay dog cartoon.

Dogbert continues to get more assertive and clever.

Debris is hard to draw.

It _would_ explain everything.

88

I'VE DECIDED TO JOIN THE ANTI-FUR MOVEMENT.

ISN'T THAT HYPOCRITICAL? YOU WEAR A FUR COAT EVERYDAY.

OH...YEAH, NEVER MIND...

WAIT...

Most issues are not black and white. I'm suspicious of anyone who has a firm belief about anything.

WE CAN SPEND THE FIRST DAY AT CLYDE CANYON HIKING AND EXPLORING...

RRRR

ARE YOU STILL MAD ABOUT THE FLIGHT ARRANGE-MENTS?

SIR, YOU'LL HAVE TO STORE YOUR CARRY-ON LUGGAGE IN THE OVER-HEAD COM-PARTMENT.

RRRR...

This is another reason Dogbert doesn't respect humans. He wouldn't put up with this now.

AH... A FULL WEEK OF HIKING AND EXPLORING.

CLYDE CANYON TRAIL

CLYDE CANYON

WE'RE GONNA BE PRETTY TIRED OF THIS PLACE BY THE END OF THE WEEK.

To me, all vacations look like this — a long hike to something that looks better in the brochure.

There's an art to taking vacations — an art I'm not good at. I always think I must be doing something wrong.

Dogbert's joy of taunting Dilbert is getting more developed now.

I wrote this in 1991. This month is the first time you can get a PCS phone in my area.

90

I had a big green pillow like this. It was great for watching TV on the floor.

DILBERT

By Scott Adams

© 1992 United Feature Syndicate, Inc.

91

My girlfriend complained about the lack of an airbag on her side.

In small ways, I revealed that Dilbert and Dogbert liked each other.

. . . Reveals His Sarcasm

If you ask me, tuxedos have too many unnecessary parts.

The art of time management is really the ability to blow people off without guilt.

Here's a glimpse of Dogbert's growth into more human preferences.

These would be
fun toys.

Dogbert increasingly comes out on top by having no ethical limitations.

My cat sits on my legs like that.

I have a friend who was a bird watcher. They're very competitive.

IF I DIED TOMORROW, WHAT WOULD YOU WRITE ON MY TOMBSTONE?

I ALWAYS ASSUMED THERE WOULD BE NO TOMBSTONE.

AH... YOU WOULD HAVE ME CREMATED.

OR STUFFED, WHICHEVER IS CHEAPER.

In 1989, I only owned one piece of new furniture. It was the green recliner chair Dogbert is in.

QUICK, QUICK! GIVE ME YOUR HAND!!!

AAACHOOO

THANKS... I ALWAYS PUT A HAND OVER MY MOUTH WHEN I SNEEZE.

My cat sneezes on me intentionally.

I CAN FEEL THE STATIC ELECTRICITY BUILDING...

SHUFFLE SHUFFLE SHUFFLE SHUFFLE

SHUFFLE SHUFFLE

SHUFFLE SHUFFLE

I MOST CERTAINLY WILL NOT CALL YOU "THOR, DOG OF THUNDER."

PREPARE TO DIE.

Thor was one of my favorite comics as a kid.

95

A lot of people don't have the capacitor for appreciating nerd puns.

I was a contestant on "Wheel of Fortune"... and lost.

why don't dogs get cavities? What's up with that?

WELL, MR. DOGBERT, WHAT COULD I DO TO CONVINCE YOU TO PUT YOUR NEW WEALTH IN OUR BANK?

STRETCH YOUR POLYESTER PANTS OVER THE TOP OF YOUR HEAD.

I HOPE MONEY DOESN'T CHANGE ME.

When I worked In a bank, we <u>hated</u> the rich customers.

KNOWLEDGE IS POWER, DOGBERT.

SOMEDAY, THE PEOPLE WHO KNOW HOW TO USE COMPUTERS WILL RULE OVER THOSE WHO DON'T.

AND THEY WILL HAVE A SPECIAL NAME FOR US.

SECRETARIES.

I had a neighbor who believed that computer skills would lead to nothing but clerical opportunities, because the computers would do the rest.

DID ANYBODY CALL ON YOUR NEW VIDEO PHONE YET?

NO.

DON'T YOU THINK THAT THE ONLY PEOPLE WHO WILL BUY VIDEO PHONES ARE MALE TECHIE DWEEBS LIKE YOU?

THEREFORE, WOULDN'T IT BE CHEAPER TO BUY A MIRROR?

IT'S HELL BEING AN EARLY ADOPTER.

I think this about Internet "chats" too.

GET IT, DOGBERT!

BLAM!

MAYBE I SHOULD JUST GET A CAT.

GOOD IDEA, BUT THEY'RE HARDER TO THROW.

Dogbert's views on the "Frisbee" concept are becoming clearer.

OUR SCHOOL SYSTEM IS A COMPLETE FAILURE, DOGBERT.

WHY'S THAT?

THE SCHOOLS SHOULD BE PREPARING THESE KIDS TO BE SCIENTISTS AND ENGINEERS. THAT'S THE ONLY WAY OUR ECONOMY WILL PROSPER.

INSTEAD, WE'LL BE A NATION OF MAIDS AND JANITORS.

YEAH, BUT THINK HOW CLEAN IT WILL BE.

I think every story has a positive side. But I got complaints from maids and janitors after this ran.

I CAN'T WAIT TO GROW UP AND GET OUT OF SCHOOL.

ACTUALLY, NORIKO, YOUR GENERATION WILL HAVE TO TAKE CLASSES AND WORK FULL-TIME YOUR WHOLE LIVES ... ASSUMING ANY JOBS EXIST.

BUT ON THE PLUS SIDE, TELEVISION WILL HAVE A THOUSAND CHANNELS.

THAT'S IT; SOMEBODY'S GOT SOME EXPLAINING TO DO!

Noriko is my girlfriend's middle name. This character is based on a kindergarten → 98 → picture of her I saw.

I felt like an observer in the land of engineers at Pacific Bell. I wasn't an engineer by training, but I worked closely with them.

I RECENTLY RECEIVED THIS ANGRY LETTER FROM A MISTER "DORK".

MR. DORK INFORMS ME THAT THE MANY PEOPLE SURNAMED DORK ARE NOT AMUSED THAT I ONCE USED THE WORD "DORKAGE." HE DEMANDS AN APOLOGY.

I APOLOGIZE TO ALL THE DORKS WHO WERE OFFENDED. I HOPE WE CAN PUT THIS BEHIND US.

Sometimes Dogbert speaks for me.

. . . the Many Occupations

THE DESIGNS FOR MY REVOLUTIONARY NEW "HOME DEFENSE SYSTEM" ARE NOW COMPLETE.

WELL, THIS IS VERY DETAILED. BUT WHERE DO YOU THINK WE CAN FIND THIS MANY "FLYING ATTACK PORCUPINES?"

JUST TRY TO GET A COMPLIMENT OUT OF THAT MAN.

My best ideas are the ones that people hate the most.

ARE YOU REALLY GOING THROUGH WITH THE UNAUTHORIZED BIOGRAPHY OF ME?

YES.

I'M UP TO THE PART WHERE JACKIE "O" AND LIZ TAYLOR FIGHT A DUEL FOR YOUR LOVE.

TRAGICALLY, NEITHER ARE AWARE THAT YOU'RE CARRYING STEVE GARVEY'S BABY!

TAP TAP TAP

Dogbert used a "Macintosh" in those days.

DAY ONE AS A SUBSTITUTE TEACHER

JENNIFER! PUT THAT FLAME-THROWER AWAY RIGHT THIS MINUTE!

EUGENE! RELEASE THOSE HOSTAGES OR I SHALL BE FORCED TO FLING THIS CHALK ERASER AT YOUR HEAD!

IS THAT A "STINGER" MISSILE LAUNCHER? WELL, I HOPE YOU BROUGHT ENOUGH FOR EVERYBODY!

I DID.

Dogbert is perfect for exploring the downsides of other occupations because he brings a surreal element to surreal situations.

OKAY, CLASS . . . PUT YOUR WEAPONS AWAY AND OPEN YOUR TV GUIDES.

TIMMY, PLEASE READ ALOUD THE PASSAGE FROM "FALCON CREST" UNDER THE FRIDAY LISTINGS.

THERE'S GOT TO BE A BETTER WAY TO TEACH SEX EDUCATION.

I'VE DECIDED TO BECOME AN AMBUSH REPORTER, LIKE MIKE WALLACE.

IS IT TRUE YOU MADE ALL OF YOUR MONEY UNETHICALLY AND YOU'RE HAVING AN AFFAIR?

YES!! YES!! HOW DID YOU FIND ME?!

YOU WERE CHOSEN RANDOMLY.

101

JUST A MOMENT, LITTLE GIRL. I'M DOGBERT, THE AMBUSH REPORTER.

IS IT TRUE THAT YOU PRETEND TO BE CUTE IN ORDER TO MANIPULATE ADULTS !!

OH, HEY, WAIT... I'M JUST KIDDING. CAN I BUY YOU SOMETHING EXPENSIVE?

SNIFF SNIFF

WELCOME TO DOGBERT'S SCHOOL FOR ASPIRING SELF-SERVICE GAS STATION ATTENDANTS.

I WILL TEACH YOU HOW TO SIT IN A LITTLE BUILDING AND DO NOTHING.

THESE SAME SKILLS CAN BE TRANSFERRED TO A CAREER IN CONGRESS OR FOTOMAT.

REALLY? FOTOMAT?!

There actually are schools for self-service gas station attendants. You probably fail if you try to pump gas.

I HEARD YOU CLOSED YOUR SCHOOL FOR SELF-SERVICE GAS STATION ATTENDANTS.

IT DIDN'T WORK OUT.

I WAS TEACHING THE SECTION ON REFOLDING MAPS ... FRUSTRATIONS WERE HIGH ... AT FIRST, THE PAPER CUTS WERE MINOR, BUT PANIC SWEPT THE ROOM.

WELL, HOW BAD COULD...

THEY'RE ALL DEAD...

I wanted to end this series, so I killed all the extras.

I GOT A JOB AS A USED CAR SALES-MAN.

DOES IT PAY WELL?

I'M NOT IN IT FOR THE MONEY. I JUST ENJOY LYING TO STRANGERS.

8-12

THIS ONE WAS OWNED BY CARLOS THE DIAMOND SMUGGLER. IT CORNERS WELL, BUT THE GAS MILEAGE IS BAD-- ALMOST AS IF IT HAS WEIGHTS HIDDEN IN THE DOOR PANELS.

Dogbert would be the perfect used car salesman.

MISTER DOGBERT, THE TOBACCO LOBBY IS VERY INTERESTED IN BUYING YOUR SENATOR.

SALE

WE'VE BEEN TAKING A BEATING FROM THE ANTI-SMOKING FASCISTS. I BLAME THE MEDIA.

8-26

WHAT WE NEED IS MORE ATTENTION ON THE POSITIVE ASPECTS OF SMOKING ... LIKE SEX APPEAL.

YES, SIR.

The spokespeople for tobacco companies always look half dead. The Surgeon General should make them put their pictures on every pack.

MISTER PRESIDENT, THERE'S ANOTHER OPENING ON THE SUPREME COURT. ONE OF THE OLD GUYS WANDERED AWAY.

I RECOMMEND NOMINATING A DOG THIS TIME. THEY TEND TO BE LOYAL AND EVERYBODY LIKES THEM.

11-25

IT'S FOR YOU... GEORGE SOME-BODY.

TAKE A MESSAGE.

I can't draw caricatures, so I hide them behind chairs if they're ⟨103⟩ real people.

This was during the Clarence Thomas senate confirmation process.

Dogbert ventures into the consulting field. He'll be there a lot.

↖ sometimes spelled "AAARGH!"

DILBERT

By Scott Adams

My babies look like old men.

105

I tend to think communication causes more problems than it solves.

If you don't work for a big company, you don't know how accurate the dialogue is.

I'LL BE REPRESENTING YOU CORPORATE EMPLOYEES IN A CLASS ACTION SUIT. YOUR COMPANY HAS SUCKED THE LIFE FORCE OUT OF YOU AND TURNED YOU INTO LITTLE RAGS.

MY FEE WILL BE ON A CONTINGENCY BASIS. THAT MEANS I GET THE ENTIRE SETTLEMENT PLUS I'LL USE YOU TO WAX MY BMW.

I'VE FOUND THE PERFECT CLIENTS.

SOUNDS FAIR.

DON'T MAKE WAVES.

When I worked in a cubicle, I felt like a little rag.

I PLAN TO USE MY NEW WEALTH TO BUILD AN AMUSEMENT PARK.

DOGBERTLAND WILL HAVE THRILLING RIDES LIKE "THE WEDGIE" AND I'LL HAVE A MAZE IN FRONT OF THE RESTROOMS.

THE CUSTOMERS WILL HATE THIS.

IF THEY WANT FUN THEY CAN BUILD THEIR OWN PARK.

The more selfish and mean that Dogbert is, the funnier he is.

I'M GOING TO START MY OWN BOOK PUBLISHING COMPANY SO I CAN REJECT PEOPLE ALL DAY LONG.

I'LL DISMISS THEIR LIFE'S WORK WITH A GESTURE AND A WITTY COMMENT.

BOTTOM LINE, I'M JUST NOT A PEOPLE PERSON.

I'VE NOTICED.

People tell me they like it when Dogbert wags.

I knew a guy named Tim who was rudely turned down by a publisher.

This was banned from at least one newspaper.

Does _anyone_ believe the concept of corporate confidentiality?

DOGBERT'S TECH SUPPORT

I THINK I KNOW WHAT YOUR PROBLEM IS...

TAKE ALL THE PARTS AND ARRANGE THEM IN NEAT PILES. NOW STAND ON YOUR CHAIR SO YOU CAN SEE ABOVE YOUR CUBICLE WALL...

NOW SHOUT "DOES ANYBODY KNOW HOW TO READ A MANUAL?"

This was a big hit with tech support people. (They despise callers.)

AS NEW OWNER OF THIS COMPANY I HEREBY BAN ALL MEETINGS OVER ONE HOUR. THE DRESS CODE IS CASUAL. STATUS REPORTS ARE OPTIONAL!

NO MORE MISSION STATEMENTS OR "VISIONS." OUR MOTTO IS "HAVE FUN, SATISFY CUSTOMERS, MAKE MONEY."

AND STOCK OPTIONS FOR ALL. zzz

WE CAN FIT FIVE MORE IN THIS CUBICLE IF WE REMOVE THE CHAIR.

This is ↑ my motto.

WE'VE GOT A LOT OF EMPTY CUBICLES BECAUSE OF DOWNSIZING.

I HIRED THE DOGBERT CONSTRUCTION COMPANY TO CONVERT PART OF THE OFFICE INTO PRISON CELLS WHICH WE'LL LEASE TO THE STATE.

SOUNDS LIKE A BIG JOB.

NAH. A LITTLE PAINT, NEW CARPET AND WE'RE THERE.

It could happen.

Sad, but often true.

Rush Limbaugh's fans attacked me for this. But Rush wasn't my target. I just thought it would be a good job for Dogbert.

People get mad when they think Dogbert's opinions are my opinions. Sometimes →110→ they are, but usually not.

Everybody got mad about that one.

. . . Schemes to Conquer the World

Someday I expect Dogbert to conquer the world.

I'm a wanna-be inventor. I'm still working on my perpetual motion ⊤⊤⊤→ machine. Ironically, I can't seem to stop.

Imagine an advanced race of aliens who talk to the average human; Do you think they'll be impressed?

Jim Davis, the author of "Garfield" asked for the original of this. I traded for one of his. At the time, it was my biggest economic gain as a cartoonist.

This cartoon captures the Dogbert attitude better than any other.

Gorby jokes don't age well.

wouldn't it be great to own an elf?

This plan could actually work.

I'M GOING TO FORM A PERSONALITY CULT TO HONOR ME.

I'LL TAKE EVERYBODY'S MONEY AND MAKE THEM WEAR BATHROBES WITH MY PICTURE ON THE BACK.

WOULDN'T IT BE CHEAPER TO BRAND THEM AND LET THEM RUN NAKED?

AS A RULE, WE'RE NOT TALKING ABOUT ATTRACTIVE PEOPLE HERE.

Do supermodels ever join cults? I don't think so.

I'M HOPING YOU WILL ACCEPT ME IN THE DOGBERT CULT.

YOU DO HAVE A STRONG RÉSUMÉ...

LOOKS LIKE YOU'VE BEEN FLEECED BY SEVERAL SPIRITUAL LEADERS ALREADY.

I THINK THAT DEMONSTRATES A COMPLETE ABSENCE OF INDEPENDENT THOUGHT.

CAN YOU CHANT?

I don't usually laugh at my own jokes, but the phrase, "Can you chant?" kills me every time I reread it.

TODAY ON "GERALDO" OUR ENTIRE SHOW IS ABOUT A DOG WHO STARTED HIS OWN CULT!

ACTUALLY, GERALDO, I DON'T KNOW WHAT YOU'RE TALKING ABOUT.

I LOVE LIVE TELEVISION.

This is why "Geraldo" is taped.

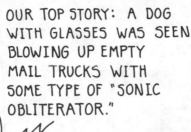

OUR TOP STORY: A DOG WITH GLASSES WAS SEEN BLOWING UP EMPTY MAIL TRUCKS WITH SOME TYPE OF "SONIC OBLITERATOR."

MUCH OF THE CITY IS IN RUINS, AS THE DOG BLASTED THROUGH BUILDINGS TO ESCAPE POLICE AND NATIONAL GUARD PURSUIT.

ON THE PLUS SIDE, WE HAVE A MUCH BETTER SHORTCUT TO THE POST OFFICE.

what happens when small weapons get more powerful? I hope I'm the first to get one on my block, while it's there.

THIS AUTHENTIC CHUNK OF THE BERLIN WALL IS THE LATEST ACQUISITION OF MY MUSEUM.

HEY! YOU MUST THINK WE'RE A COUPLE OF HILLBILLIES. WE SAW A HOLE IN YOUR SIDEWALK IN THAT EXACT SHAPE.

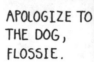

OBVIOUSLY WE HAD TO TRADE A CHUNK OF OUR SIDEWALK TO BERLIN SO WE COULD GET THIS.

APOLOGIZE TO THE DOG, FLOSSIE.

I have a chunk of the Berlin wall.
I mean, I think I have one.

WHEN I CONQUER THE EARTH... WILL IT BE MORE EFFICIENT TO PUT ALL HUMANS IN PRISON...

...OR TRAIN THEM AS DOMESTIC SERVANTS FOR DOGS?

IT'S AMAZING HOW DOGS CAN SIT FOR HOURS THINKING ABSOLUTELY NOTHING.

what do you think they're thinking about?

DILBERT

By Scott Adams

WHY DO DOGS TWITCH THEIR FEET WHEN THEY SLEEP?

ZZZZ

IT'S SO CUTE. THEY MUST BE DREAMING ABOUT CHASING CARS.

HA HA! I AM SAINT DOGBERT! LINE UP TO KISS MY FEET, YOU KNAVES!

WHAT'S ON MY SCHEDULE TODAY, LACKEY?

YOU'LL BE PUSHING WHINEY, UGLY PEOPLE INTO MUD AT NINE.

7-14

THEN, YOU'LL TEASE CATS ABOUT THEIR GROOMING METHODS UNTIL TEN.

GOOD, GOOD.

THEN YOU'LL RAISE TAXES, GO TO LUNCH, AND TAKE THE REST OF THE DAY OFF.

© 1991 United Feature Syndicate, Inc.

REALITY: WHAT A GYP.

This is what I dream about too.

118

I'll bet some readers went into spontaneous zombie mode when they read this.

Who makes the rules about who can touch other creatures and how? It all seems kinda arbitrary to me.

This joke made sense in 1992. Trust me.

WHAT'S THIS?

I'M STARTING MY OWN NEWSLETTER FOR CLUELESS PEOPLE.

THANKS TO THE TECHNICAL MARVEL OF DESKTOP PUBLISHING, CLUELESS PEOPLE WILL NOW HAVE THE BENEFIT OF MY IMMENSE WISDOM.

HOW DO YOU KNOW WHO THE CLUELESS PEOPLE ARE?

THEY ASK A LOT OF QUESTIONS.

Shouldn't there be a newsletter for the clueless?

BOB, HERE'S A COPY OF MY NEW NEWSLETTER FOR CLUELESS PEOPLE.

"DOGBERT'S CLUES FOR THE CLUELESS:
1. PROFESSIONAL WRESTLING IS ALL FAKED.
2. NOBODY EVER LOST WEIGHT ON A HOME EXERCISE DEVICE."

" 3. LOOKS ARE MORE IMPORTANT TO HAPPINESS THAN BRAINS
4. IF PEOPLE DON'T COMMENT ON YOUR NEW HAIRDO, THEY HATE IT."

IT'S NOT HEALTHY TO READ THEM ALL AT ONCE, BOB.

IT'S A MIRACLE, RATBERT. THE IMAGE OF SAINT TED APPEARED IN MY JAR OF PEANUT BUTTER!

SAINT TED? WHO EVER HEARD OF SAINT TED? COULDN'T YOU GET SAINT THERESA?

SHE WAS BOOKED TO A CAN OF VARNISH IN UPSTATE NEW YORK.

SAINT TED LOOKS LIKE A "HAPPY FACE."

If there's a Hell, I'm going there for sure.

"ALTHOUGH RAISING CHILDREN IS DIFFICULT, BE ASSURED THAT YOU WILL GET HELP FROM A POWER GREATER THAN YOURSELF."

"TEACH YOUR CHILDREN ABOUT THE HIGHER POWER AND ABOUT THE 'GREAT BOOK' WHICH WILL GIVE THEM DIRECTION."

THEY'RE CALLED "TV LISTINGS." WITHOUT THEM, YOU'RE JUST FLIPPING.

Is that the ugliest baby you ever saw?

LOOKS EASY ENOUGH.

HYPNOSIS FOR WORLD CONQUEST

HI, DOGBERT! WHAT ARE YOU READING?

NOTHING. YOU WILL REMEMBER NOTHING

WHO AM I? WHERE AM I?

THAT WAS A LITTLE BIT LIKE SAND-BLASTING A SOUP CRACKER.

If hypnosis worked, wouldn't all the leaders be hypnotists? What if they are?

THIS IS DOGBERT... YOU ARE ALL UNDER MY HYPNOTIC POWERS...

I AM THE SUPREME RULER OF EARTH. YOU MUST ALL CARRY DOGBERT POSTERS AND CHANT "DOGBERT IS MY KING."

THAT IS ALL FOR NOW. IF I THINK OF ANYTHING ELSE IMPORTANT I'LL LET YOU KNOW.

...IS MY KING

I favor the "Playful Despot" form of government.

If I ever understand why people collect plates, I will know everything there is to know about people.

I'd buy it.

Dogbert continues to get aggressive. Here he's channeling the personality of a loud co-worker from my cubicle days.

Have you ever insisted on carefully reading a petition before signing? It makes the **123** gatherers nervous.

This concept is based on an ex-co-worker's philosophy. It worked quite well.

Here's a story line that wasn't as fun on paper as it was in my head...

...But I was working my day job and couldn't afford to throw the cartoon out and 124 do another. So I confessed.

. . . Saving Dilbert

DILBERT HIRES A CLEANING PERSON

AND YOUR NAME IS..?

CALL ME MR. TIDY.

THE AGENCY SAYS YOU'RE EXPERIENCED.

YEAH, I'VE CLEANED OUT SOME OF THE NICER HOMES IN THIS AREA

THE BEST THING HERE IS TO LOAD YOUR POSSESSIONS INTO MY VAN, AND I'LL CLEAN 'EM AT MY PLACE.

WILL THAT COST ME EXTRA?

I try to make the criminals non-stereotypical and caucasian so I don't get beat up.

DOGBERT, WHERE'S ALL OF OUR FURNITURE?!!

YOUR NEW CLEANING PERSON LOADED IT INTO HIS VAN AND DROVE AWAY... OH, AND HE SAID TO TELL YOU HE QUIT.

I THINK WE NEED TO REVIEW YOUR JOB DESCRIPTION AS WATCH DOG.

I GOT HIS ADDRESS.

SEND MY CHECK TO 1348 OKE WALNUT T...

Dogbert only <u>seems</u> non-dangerous.

DILBERT THE VIGILANTE

WHEN I GET HOME FROM WORK, WE'LL TRACK DOWN THE MAN WHO ROBBED OUR HOUSE AND MAKE HIM PAY!!

NO! IT'S THE ROBBER AT MY DESK. HE'S STEALING MY JOB TOO!

HE'S AN IMPOSTER. LOOK AT HIS HAIR!

WE THOUGHT YOU'D BEEN IN A STREET FIGHT WITH VIDAL SASSOON.

A reader told me that Vidal Sassoon was actually a tough character in his wilder youth. I don't know if it's true.

This was my version of a touching "Lassie" plot.

Ultimately, Dogbert will always rescue Dilbert.

Remember, stalagmites might hang from the ceiling, but they don't.

126

I have to turn the paper upside down to draw Dilbert upside down.

I love to write dialogue for two characters who are equally defective but in different ways.

I got lots of mail about this one. Many people didn't understand it. others **127** loved it.

This is the very first Ratbert appearance. I wasn't planning to make him a regular.

This is based loosely on the old "frogs with no legs are deaf" joke.

Sometimes it's hard to review the plot so you can get to the next joke.

Ratbert was an unplanned addition to the **Dilbert** cast. It all started with one series of jokes about a gullible lab rat who thought he was being fed massive amounts of food simply because the scientist was a polite host.

Ratbert's scientist could only afford one rat because of budget cutbacks. That meant that he had to keep Ratbert alive from one experiment to the next. (It also meant I didn't have to draw a lot of rat "extras" standing around in the scene.)

I like to keep my characters on the edge of awareness about their situation. In this case Ratbert was starting to get suspicious about the motives of the scientist. His innocence and exuberance were personally amusing to me and easy to write. The challenge was integrating him with Dilbert's household.

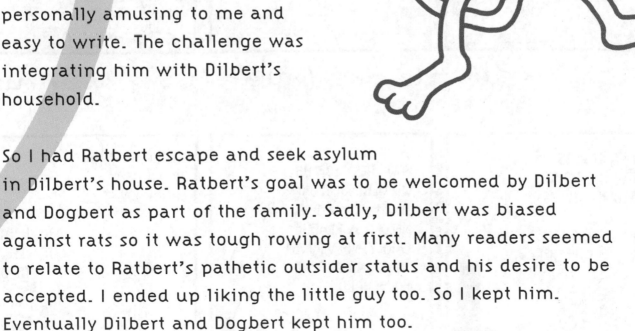

So I had Ratbert escape and seek asylum in Dilbert's house. Ratbert's goal was to be welcomed by Dilbert and Dogbert as part of the family. Sadly, Dilbert was biased against rats so it was tough rowing at first. Many readers seemed to relate to Ratbert's pathetic outsider status and his desire to be accepted. I ended up liking the little guy too. So I kept him. Eventually Dilbert and Dogbert kept him too.

At first, Ratbert can't imagine why anyone would be prejudiced against rats.

I often felt like Ratbert in my cubicle maze.

Dilbert is particularly closed-minded about rats.

Ratbert was the first "bert" after Dogbert, thus establishing a pattern.

Ratbert is prejudiced against mice.

Here's a good trivia question: what was Ratbert's original name? **131**

A SCIENTIST REPORTS THAT LOVE MADE A LAB RAT STUPID.

THE SCIENTIST CAUTIONED THE MEDIA NOT TO DRAW CONCLUSIONS BASED ON ONE RAT.

TIME

LOVE AND S.A.T. SCORES

If it weren't for lack of context, there would be no news.

THERE'S A TERRIBLE STIGMA TO BEING A RAT...

I ONCE PAINTED A POUCH ON MY STOMACH AND TOLD PEOPLE I WAS A TINY KANGA-ROO

THAT'S WHEN I FOUND OUT THAT PEOPLE HATE TINY KANGAROOS.

Don't you love the phrase "Tiny kangaroos"?

ALL THIS WEEK I'VE BEEN TESTING MADONNA'S "COMPULSION" PERFUME AT THE LAB.

ANY SIDE EFFECTS?

HECK NO... UNLESS YOU CONSIDER MARRYING A BUNSEN BURNER A "SIDE EFFECT."

SAY...WHO'S THAT CUTE LITTLE FILLY ON THE TABLE?!

WE CALL HER THE LAMP.

132

what if perfume actually did what it promised?

WHAT DO YOU THINK OF MY CHIHUAHUA DISGUISE?!

IT'S A GOOD START, RATBERT, BUT IT TAKES MORE THAN A TURTLENECK TO LOOK LIKE A CHIHUAHUA.

HOW ABOUT IF I MAKE THIS FACE AND ACT NERVOUS?

PERFECT.

⌐ words to live by.

WHY DOES DOGBERT ALWAYS GET TO SIT ON YOUR LEGS AND I NEVER DO?

BECAUSE DOGBERT IS MY BEST FRIEND AND YOU'RE JUST A DISEASE-CARRYING VERMIN.

MAYBE THIS ISN'T THE TIME TO LAUNCH MY "FAMILY HUG TIME" CONCEPT.

Ratbert begins the full-court press for family acceptance.

FORGET DOGBERT; I CAN BE YOUR NEW BEST FRIEND!

RATS ARE TWICE AS GOOD FOR CUDDLING. AND YOU SHOULD SEE ME CATCH A FRISBEE!

HERE, SCRATCH BEHIND MY EARS. YOU'LL FIND ME MOST APPRECIATIVE!

YOU SOUND LIKE ME ON A DATE.

I'm surprised I got away with this one.

Ratbert got bigger because it was easier to draw him that way around the other characters.

I WAS WONDERING IF WE'RE A DYSFUNCTIONAL FAMILY.

YOU'RE NOT A FAMILY MEMBER. YOU'RE A RAT WHO WON'T GO AWAY.

SUDDENLY I HAVE THE URGE TO ROB A CONVENIENCE STORE.

Ratbert is easy to write for because he's so cute. Anything he says sounds funnier because of that.

WHAT ARE THOSE DISHES DOING ON DILBERT'S HEAD?

HE'S IN A VIDEO GAME TRANCE. I'M TESTING MY THEORY THAT HE IS UNAWARE OF HIS ENVIRONMENT AND HAS NO DISCERNABLE MENTAL ACTIVITY.

POOR GUY.

WHAT A TEAM WE MAKE, BOB!

NOW I WON'T NEED TO ACT PATHETIC TO GET LOVE. I'LL GET ALL THE SPILLOVER LOVE THAT PEOPLE NATURALLY HAVE FOR DINOSAURS!

EWW! IT'S A HUGE LIZARD WITH A TALKING ZIT. I'M GONNA BE SICK.

GREAT... I GOT A DEFECTIVE DINOSAUR.

Paired with Bob The Dinosaur, there's almost too much cuteness.

135

Things are looking bad for Ratbert...

Finally, Ratbert is accepted in the family.

Like any family member, Ratbert is free to be annoying.

SINCE YOU WON'T GO AWAY, I'LL MAKE YOU AN INTERN.

GREAT! WHAT'S AN INTERN?

YOU'LL SPEND YOUR DAY IN A HIGH-TRAFFIC CUBE TRYING TO LOOK BUSY. YOUR MAIN FUNCTION IS TO MAKE THE REST OF US GLAD WE'RE NOT YOU.

© 1994 United Feature Syndicate, Inc.

12-16

HOW DID PEOPLE EVER LOOK BUSY BEFORE COMPUTERS?

Ratbert is perfect for low-ego jobs.

I'M GOING TO INTERVIEW SUCCESSFUL PEOPLE AND WRITE A BOOK OF THEIR TIPS. I'LL START WITH YOU, DOGBERT.

SET YOUR ALARM CLOCK TO GO OFF EVERY HOUR. KEEP A BIG VAT OF "JELL-O" BY THE BED. WHEN THE ALARM GOES OFF, STICK YOUR HEAD IN THE "JELL-O" AND YELL "BOY, I'M TIRED!"

© 1995 United Feature Syndicate, Inc. (NYC)

5/3

THANKS!

BEWARE THE ADVICE OF SUCCESSFUL PEOPLE; THEY DO NOT SEEK COMPANY.

Do you think successful people tell **all** of their secrets?

MY INSPIRATIONAL POSTERS AREN'T WORKING. I NEED TO DO SOME ANIMAL RESEARCH, RATBERT.

READY!!

IN THIS BEAUTIFUL SCENE WE SEE A MIGHTY EAGLE SWOOPING DOWN TO CAPTURE ITS PREY. WHAT IS YOUR REACTION?

© 1995 United Feature Syrdicate, Inc.(NYC)

9/6

I THINK IT'S WORKING.

RUN FOR IT, MOM!!!

Has anyone **ever** been inspired by a poster?

I like the idea of geniuses existing around us in unlikely professions.

If a genius does something that doesn't make sense to me, why do I think he's wrong?

GARBAGEMAN

Dilbert's **Garbageman** is the world's smartest human. I like putting incongruous things together. The unanswered question about this character is why he would choose to be a garbageman if he was the smartest man in the world. But if you think about it, we wouldn't be in a position to judge anything done by the world's smartest person. Obviously his decisions would be different from our own—he's smarter! So if we don't understand why he does what he does, the problem is probably on our end.

MAYBE I'LL NEVER SOLVE THE MYSTERY OF WHY DILBERT'S NECKTIES CURL UP.

SOMETIMES, DOGBERT, LIFE PRESENTS US WITH MYSTERIES TO FUEL OUR SENSE OF WONDER... IT STIMULATES US TO REACH BEYOND OURSELVES TO SOMETHING GREATER.

© 1991 United Feature Syndicate, Inc.

THIS ISN'T ONE OF THOSE TIMES, IS IT?

APPARENTLY NOT.

I knew a garbage man who found great stuff in the trash and fixed it up. He was literally smarter than his customers in almost every way. I admired him.

I WISH YOU'D REALIZE THAT YOU'RE A GARBAGE MAN, NOT AN ENGINEER. I DON'T NEED YOUR SUGGESTIONS ON MY DESIGNS.

WHAT ARE YOU WRITING? OH YEAH, AS IF I CARE.

IF YOU NEED HELP UNDERSTANDING THAT, THE PAPER BOY WILL BE BY SOON. I'VE BEEN WORKING WITH HIM.

I get many suggestions from non-cartoonists. The worst part is that many of them are good.

DILBERT WON'T BUILD A PHASER PISTOL FOR ME. HE THINKS IT'S WRONG TO ZAP PEOPLE FOR FUN.

YEAH, THAT WOULD BE WRONG... UNLESS THE PEOPLE YOU ZAP ARE THEMSELVES IMMORAL, IN WHICH CASE YOU WOULD BE ON THE SIDE OF JUSTICE.

I GUESS IT'S ACADEMIC SINCE I DON'T HAVE A PHASER.

HERE, BORROW MINE.

I wish I had a phaser.

141

I played in a co-ed soccer league. We lost every game. I kept watching my teammates instead of the ball.

I wanted Liz to look athletic, but she looks 12 years old.

Hey, It's hard to draw soccer balls! You try it.

142

LIZ

I created **Liz** so Dilbert could experience having a girlfriend. Liz is a materials engineer and a good soccer player. She likes brainy guys and she has very big hair. That's all we know about her.

Many readers asked me to allow Dilbert to lose his innocence with Liz, so to speak. But I didn't see any way I could do that in a comic strip and get it past the editors. So I developed a secret sign. I told the people who receive the **Dilbert** newsletter that if Dilbert ever got lucky with Liz, I would draw his normally upturned necktie flat one day. I expected a flood of e-mail from people encouraging me to do it.

I was wrong.

The women who wrote were almost unanimous in their desire for Dilbert to get lucky. But the men were split evenly. Half wanted Dilbert to do the deed and half said, in effect, "I don't think Dilbert should get lucky until I do."

Apparently a large segment of the male population was using Dilbert as a yardstick of their own success with women and they didn't want to fall any further behind.

Now I had a problem.

I ended up finessing the situation by writing a strip with an intentionally ambiguous ending. Everyone had the option of thinking his view prevailed. Here is the lead up to the flat tie strip.

My biggest problem with Liz is that I'm not very good at drawing attractive female characters. People told me she looked twelve years old. And she never really clicked with me or the readers, so I eventually gave up on her and had her break up with Dilbert. I don't know if she'll be back.

I liked the concept of Liz being a science wonk.

THIS WAS OUR THIRD DATE, LIZ. TRADITION DEMANDS THAT YOU KISS ME OR GIVE ME THE "LET'S BE FRIENDS" TALK.

7-2

NO, OUR FIRST DATE ONLY COUNTED AS 85% OF A DATE BECAUSE WE WERE WEARING OUR SWEAT PANTS.

I'M 15% SHORT?!!

IT'S TOO BAD, BECAUSE I REALLY FELT LIKE KISSING.

© 1994 United Feature Syndicate, Inc.

Everyone understands the third date rule, right?

IT SEEMS ALMOST UNNATURAL FOR ME TO HAVE AN ACTUAL GIRLFRIEND.

WHY?

IT'S LIKE WHEN THE CAPTAIN ON "STAR TREK" FALLS IN LOVE, AND YOU KNOW THE WOMAN WILL DIE IN AN UNLIKELY ACCIDENT.

HEY! WE JUST SAW OUR FIRST SHOOTING STAR!

© 1994 United Feature Syndicate, Inc.

7-25

I was toying with the idea of bumping Liz off, but this was as close as it got.

LIZ, IF YOU'RE GOING TO CONTINUE SEEING DILBERT, YOU'LL HAVE TO PASS MY TEST.

QUESTION ONE: GIVE SEVEN HUNDRED REASONS WHY DOGS ARE SUPERIOR TO CATS.

11-25

WELL, THE FIRST SIX HUNDRED REASONS HAVE TO DO WITH THE FACT THAT YOU'RE CUTER.

FINGERNAILS! SHE-DEVIL!

© 1994 United Feature Syndicate, Inc.

Liz would have to be acceptable to Dogbert.

Panel 1:
I BUILT A SPREADSHEET TO COMPARE OUR RELATIVE QUALITIES. I'M AFRAID I'M TWENTY PERCENT TOO GOOD FOR YOU. WE MUST STOP DATING.

Panel 2:
NO! LOOK, LIZ, YOU HAVE THE WRONG FORMULA IN THIS COLUMN! THAT MUST MEAN I HAVE HIGHER MATH SKILLS THAN YOU! WE'RE ALMOST EVEN!

Panel 3:
YOU LEFT THAT ERROR IN THERE INTENTIONALLY.

MY LAST BATCH OF FLOWERS IS WILTING.

Liz had to like Dilbert's nerdiness or the relationship made no sense.

I'M SO LUCKY TO BE DATING YOU, LIZ. YOU'RE AT LEAST AN EIGHT.

YOU'RE A TEN.

ARE WE USING THE SAME SCALE?

TEN IS THE NUMBER OF SECONDS IT WOULD TAKE TO REPLACE YOU.

I suspect this scene has happened a million times in real life.

Panel 7:
I THINK YOU LIKE THAT COMPUTER MORE THAN YOU LIKE ME.

Panel 8:
THAT'S NOT TRUE, LIZ. I DO NOT LIKE THAT COMPUTER MORE THAN I LIKE YOU.

Panel 9:
PLEASE, PLEASE DON'T ASK ABOUT THE LAPTOP.

"THAT" COMPUTER?

I have the cutest little laptop. I love that thing.

© 1995 United Feature Syndicate, Inc. (NYC)

what about me? I drew a cartoon about reading a book about a simulation...

Why is the floor more comfortable than the couch?

IN THE YEAR THAT WE'VE DATED, LIZ, YOU'VE OFTEN MENTIONED VARIOUS PROBLEMS IN YOUR LIFE.

I HAVE COMPILED THOSE PROBLEMS INTO A LIST OF REQUIREMENTS AND DEVELOPED A COMPREHENSIVE SET OF SOLUTIONS.

HOW THOUGHTFUL. I DIDN'T EVEN KNOW I WAS BROKEN.

NO, NO, NOT BROKEN... JUST A BIT BUGGY.

The end is near.

I'VE DECIDED TO DATE OTHER MEN.

NOOO!!! DON'T BREAK UP WITH ME!

I'M NOT. I JUST WANT TO DATE OTHER MEN AT THE SAME TIME.

I AM **NOT** HAPPY RIGHT NOW.

THAT'S EXACTLY WHY I NEED A SPARE.

I know a woman who threatened her boy-friend by saying she would get an "additional" boyfriend.

LIZ STARTED DATING OTHER MEN. TWO CAN PLAY AT THAT GAME.

I WILL USE THE POWER OF THE INTERNET TO FIND A HOT BABE.

AH! HERE'S ONE.

SHE WANTS YOUR CREDIT CARD NUMBER.

OOH! SHE'S INQUISITIVE. I LIKE THAT.

People wrote to 150 warn me that chocolate is dangerous for dogs.

MOM & DAD

Mom and Dad Dilbert's mother—"The Dilmom," as some readers call her—is one of my favorite characters. She gives us an idea where Dilbert got his skill with technology. On the outside she's a cookie-baking, fifties sort of woman. But she reveals in small glimpses an incredible depth of technical skill and understanding.

Dilbert's father has never been seen in the strip, only referred to. He has been at the all-you-can-eat restaurant in the local mall for years. He won't leave until it's "all he can eat." The restaurant is open 24 hours a day so it has been a standoff so far. Dilbert gets his brains from his mother's side and his literalness from his dad. Put them together and you have a perfect engineer.

151

You just need lots of them.

That's her hair, not a weird hat.

I CAN'T BELIEVE YOUR FATHER HAS BEEN LOST AT THE MALL SINCE 1992!

IF MY FATHER OR MY HUSBAND WERE LOST AT THE MALL I'D BE SEARCHING FOR HIM TWENTY-FOUR HOURS A DAY!!

WE'RE WAITING FOR A SALE.

YOU'RE A BIT OF A WHINER, AREN'T YOU, DEAR?

You can't tell if they're pulling Liz's leg. Even I don't know.

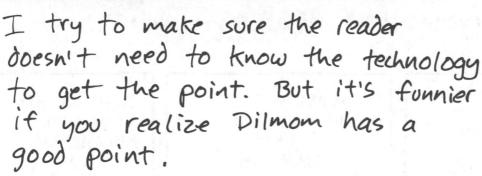

MY COMPANY ASKED ALL EMPLOYEES TO ACT AS SALESPEOPLE TO FRIENDS AND FAMILY. I THINK YOU COULD USE THIS, MOM.

WHY WOULD I NEED A PRIMARY RATE CIRCUIT? I'VE ALREADY GOT A FRAME RELAY DROP TO MY WEB SERVER IN THE SEWING ROOM.

THIS IS GOING TO BE A TOUGH SALE.

HELLO-O-O! EARTH TO DILBERT! THIS IS PACKET DATA...

I try to make sure the reader doesn't need to know the technology to get the point. But it's funnier if you realize Dilmom has a good point.

MY COMPUTER SIMULATION WILL DETERMINE, ONCE AND FOR ALL, THE REAL REASON DINOSAURS BECAME EXTINCT.

7-17

WAIT... ACCORDING TO THIS, IT WOULD BE ALMOST IMPOSSIBLE FOR ALL DINOSAURS TO BE EXTINCT.

THEN THEY MUST JUST BE...

S.Adams

...HIDING.

YEAH? JUST TRY TO FIND US.

SHHHH!

© 1989 United Feature Syndicate, Inc.

The strip wasn't doing too well in 1989, so I was looking for a hook to draw people in.

HEY... YOU WERE RIGHT. DINOSAURS AREN'T EXTINCT.

I'M BOB. SHE'S DAWN. WE WERE HIDING IN YOUR HOUSE.

ONLY ONE KIND OF DINOSAUR COULD HIDE THAT WELL...

CORRECT: A NOBODYSAURUS.

© 1989 United Feature Syndicate, Inc.

7-19 S.Adams

Everyone loves dinosaurs, right?

...SO DAWN HERE IS A NOBODYSAURUS, AND BOB, YOU SAY YOU'RE A THESAURUS?

7-20

HA HA! NO, THE "THESAURUS" LINE IS JUST AN OLD DINOSAUR JOKE.

HEE HEE!

© 1989 United Feature Syndicate, Inc.

I'LL BET YOU WERE A RIOT IN THE MESOZOIC ERA.

EAT HIM, BOB.

S.Adams

Dawn is the name of a friend of mine who has non-human thoughts on a regular basi

DINOSAURS

Bob, Dawn, and Rex the Dinosaurs emerged

after Dilbert calculated it was impossible for all dinosaurs to be extinct—therefore they must be hiding. And they were, in people's houses. Dinosaurs turned out to be smaller than we thought and able to hide very effectively.

Bob and Dawn were the two dinosaurs living in Dilbert's house. Later they gave birth to little Rex. Bob is dumb and easily excited. His favorite activity is giving wedgies to people who deserve it. His character is more fun than Dawn or Rex, so you won't see much of Bob's family. They continue to hide.

OKAY THEN, IF YOU TWO DINOSAURS WANT TO CONTINUE HIDING IN MY HOUSE YOU HAVE TO OBSERVE THE HOUSE RULES.

LET'S SEE...UH...REMAIN OUT OF SIGHT...DON'T LEAVE THE LIGHTS ON WHEN YOU'RE OUT OF THE ROOM...

S. Adams

© 1989 United Feature Syndicate, Inc.

AM I FORGETTING ANYTHING, DOGBERT?

HOW ABOUT "NO RIPPING THE FLESH OFF THE OTHER RESI-DENTS."

A rare action sequence.

I used to have that problem.

If nobody taught humans how to mate, could they figure it out on their own?

The reference desk librarian knows everything!

Dinosaurs invite dumb jokes. It's not my fault.

I'm glad I wasn't born in an egg. It looks uncomfortable.

Rex is the name I would give myself if that were a graceful option.

Yikes! I just realized today is Father's Day and I haven't called home yet! (Really)

I stopped listening to adults when I was about ten. I still don't.

159

DILBERT
By Scott Adams

ADD ONE JAR OF SPAGHETTI SAUCE...

HMPH
GRRR
UNH

RRRRR

LET ME TRY TO HUMIL-IATE YOU BY OPENING IT EASILY.

THIS DEFINITELY WOULD HAVE WORKED IN "FAMILY CIRCUS."

I'LL SEE IF BOB CAN OPEN IT.

NO PROBLEM FOR A MIGHTY DINOSAUR.

6-23

SMASH!

WILL YOU STOP HUMMING "MY WAY."

S. Adams

Maybe Bob is a "Wedgie-sore-ass."

The tongue really sells this one.

RATBERT THE OPTIMIST

I FEEL LUCKY TODAY.

LUCKY, LUCKY, LUCKY.

I THINK A HAT JUST BLEW ONTO MY HEAD!!

This is the first appearance of catbert.

BOB, I'LL YANK THE CAT OFF OF RATBERT'S HEAD AND YOU STOMP ON IT!

YANK
STOMP

I COULD HAVE PHRASED THAT BETTER.

I'M NOT AN OPTIMIST ANYMORE.

YOU'RE NOT WELCOME HERE, CAT. IT'S AGAINST HOUSE RULES TO EAT RATBERT.

MY WORK HERE IS NOT DONE UNTIL I HAVE POUNCED ON MY NATURAL ENEMY.

WHO ARE YOU, AND WHAT ARE YOU DOING ON MY KEYBOARD?

Cat owners understand that cats love to get on keyboards. Other people were confused by this one.

CATBERT

Catbert was introduced for one series of strips involving an attack on Ratbert. I had no plans to keep the cat character. When readers saw him they wrote hundreds of e-mail messages requesting "more Catbert." The funny thing was, I had not named this character, yet everyone referred to him as Catbert. It seems to me that when hundreds of readers spontaneously and unanimously name a character for you, it's a good idea to keep him.

The challenge was figuring out how to integrate Catbert into the **Dilbert** world. I didn't want him to live under Dogbert's roof, and most of the action was happening in Dilbert's office. One day in the shower, inspiration came. I decided to make Catbert the Director of Human Resources at Dilbert's company. It's the perfect fit. Like H.R. directors, cats don't care if you live or die. And they enjoy playing with you before downsizing you.

Catbert is fashioned after my fat gray cat, Freddie.

I worried that adding a cat was not very original. But then I realized nothing else in the strip was original either, so I got over it.

Catbert has become a virtual mascot for Human Resources employees.

Those aren't stripes on his back, just shading.

I know the concept of dress codes was invented by a cat.

who decided that jeans are not business clothes?
It seems like a random decision to me.

Many employees have been plagued by "dotted line" bosses. I know I was. **166**

The "Total Compensation" concept is pulled from real life. It sounds much →**167**→ better than "pay cut."

OH GOOD, THE LAST STOP OF THE DAY.

FREEZE, MORTAL! LET ME SEE THE EXPIRATION DATE ON THAT MILK!

I CAN GO TO HELL FOR DRINKING OLD MILK?!

NAH. I'M FROM "HECK." WE HANDLE THE LITTLE STUFF.

This is the first strip with Phil, The Prince of Insufficient light.

GOSH. I THOUGHT "HECK" WAS JUST A FIGURE OF SPEECH.

YEAH. A LOT OF PEOPLE THINK THEY CAN GET AWAY WITH MINOR INFRACTIONS.

ACCORDING TO MY RECORDS, LAST MONTH YOU DELIBERATELY ASKED FOR THREE LITTLE KETCHUPS AT McDONALD'S WHEN YOU KNEW YOU ONLY NEEDED TWO.

I KNEW THAT WOULD COME BACK TO HAUNT ME. LOOK, I STILL HAVE THE EXTRA ONE. I'LL GIVE IT BACK!

SHAME SHAME...

Can you tell he's holding a big spoon? It's not as scary as a pitchfork.

GEE, IF YOU'RE THE RULER OF "HECK" YOU MUST HAVE SOME KIND OF AWESOME NAME.

YEAH.

WELL, WHAT IS IT? SOMETHING LIKE "KING OF EVIL" OR "LORD OF DARKNESS"?

YOU CAN CALL ME PHIL, PRINCE OF INSUFFICIENT LIGHT.

Phil, The Prince of Insufficient Light

In my first year of syndication I tried to introduce Satan as a regular member of the **Dilbert** cast. My editor at United Media wisely advised against anything that would make me look like a Satan-worshiping cartoonist. (It doesn't take many complaints for a newspaper editor to decide to drop a new strip.) But I really wanted the devil character so I argued my case. After some negotiations, I ended up compromising and softening the character to its current form—Phil, Ruler of Heck, Prince of Insufficient Light. He wouldn't damn you, but he might darn you for minor infractions.

Oddly enough, the stripped-down, compromised version of Satan was much more interesting than the real thing would have been. So I'm quite pleased with the result. And to date I have not been accused of being in league with Phil, so it all worked out.

Many people who started reading **Dilbert** after Phil's introduction were confused by his occasional appearance. A number of people noted the facial similarity to the Pointy-Haired Boss and wondered if he was related. In truth, I just can't draw that many different faces, but I liked the suggestion that they might be brothers. And so it was revealed that in fact they are. I'm nothing if not flexible.

169

Sometimes Phil has a cape because I forget he isn't supposed to have one. **170**

171

There's that cape again! And I forgot the spoon!

I even forgot to make his tail unpointy.

A <u>lot</u> of readers were confused by this strip. They hadn't seen Phil for a long time and the spoon was drawn so poorly it wasn't recognizable.

Here I was using a computer font for lettering, which is a minor sin itself.

Phil's jowl lines have disappeared, just as the boss's did.

The brothers have a reunion.

I argued with my editor that nobody would think this cartoon is →173→ obscene.

Asok is named after a friend of mine from Pacific Bell. A more common spelling is Ashok.

I remember my own gradual increase in awareness about the work world.

I spelled "Jeffries" tube wrong. I was guessing.

ASOK

Asok, pronounced ah-shook, was introduced to satisfy the hordes of interns who wrote to request their own character. Asok is brilliant, but as an intern he is immensely naive about the cruelties and politics of the business world. The regular cast members have fun at his expense, as is common with most interns.

Asok is from India, but I haven't mentioned that in the strip yet. Only the name gives it away. Prior to Asok, I had intentionally avoided any racial diversity in the primary cast because I only like characters who have huge, gaping character flaws. The world is far too sensitive to let me get away with a highly flawed minority member.

Asok was a good way to tiptoe into the diversity water and test the temperature. Asok's only flaw is his lack of experience, which is obviously temporary. That's as cautious as you can get. But predictably, I have been flamed to a crisp for my alleged "negative stereotype of people from India."

I'm keeping Asok, flames and all. And if I get any more complaints I think I'll turn him into a drug smuggler. I've never been good at playing defense.

Men <u>do</u> have an instinct about unnecessary work.
It only <u>looks</u> like we're lazy.

Fortunately, my publishers think this is funny.

Probably half of the people who read this didn't realize 40% is exactly normal. Others thought I didn't realize it.

Some readers did tests and found out that small fonts do save space, but not much.

Technical Writers **178** get no respect.

Tina the Technical Writer

Do you know anyone who takes personal offense at everything you say, even if you're talking about the weather? I do. That's why I created Tina—to vent some of my frustration at people like that. I labeled her "brittle" as a short-hand for her tendency to be easily offended.

I wanted some gender balance in the strip so I made Tina female. And in order for Tina to fit into Dilbert's office I needed to give her a job. So I made her a Technical Writer. (The job involves translating technical jargon into clear writing for instruction manuals, technical reports, and that sort of thing. Most engineering offices have at least one Technical Writer.)

When Tina first appeared in the strip my e-mail turned into a river of flame. Technical Writers blasted me for maligning their profession. Women and men alike blasted me for what many considered a negative stereotype of women.

I knew I had a winner here.

I was fascinated by the accusations that Tina was a "too stereotypical" female character. It raises a couple of interesting questions:

1. Who says "brittle" is a female stereotype?

2. Is it possible to create a nonstereotypical character?

179

Apparently there's a list of stereotypes somewhere and under the female column is the word "brittle." I was unaware of this list. I can't say it squares with my own observations.

My mother was my most formative female influence. She was born of farmer stock. Mom could put a bullet through a deer's forehead at 300 yards, and did. In fact, she kept a loaded rifle behind the kitchen door to blast bunny rabbits that ventured near our garden. When she wasn't gunning down innocent mammals she was hitting baseballs to my brother and me, or beating us in tennis, or tooling around on her motorcycle.

So what is this "brittle" thing I keep hearing about?

Okay, let's say the critics are right and Tina is "too stereotypical." That brings us to the next question. What would a nonstereotypical character be like? As someone from China once warned: "Be careful what you wish for. You might get it."

Just to stir up trouble, I created Antina (the ANtidote to TINA). Antina didn't dress like a stereotypical woman, didn't talk like a stereotypical woman, didn't have a body like a stereotypical woman, and didn't have stereotypical female interests.

My e-mail caught on fire again. This time I was accused of making fun of lesbians. Obviously there was no safe ground in this game.

After I had my fun I got rid of Antina—she was a one joke character—but I kept Tina and will be broadening her personality over time. That's the only antidote to accusations of stereotyping, but it takes awhile to get there.

TINA, YOU'LL HAVE TO HAVE ALL THE DOCUMENTATION WRITTEN BY NEXT WEEK SO WE CAN SHIP IT WHEN THE SOFTWARE IS DONE.

HOW CAN I WRITE INSTRUCTIONS FOR SOMETHING THAT DOESN'T EXIST YET?

YOU'LL HAVE TO MAKE LOGICAL GUESSES.

"IF YOU PRESS ANY KEY YOUR COMPUTER WILL LOCK UP. IF YOU CALL OUR TECH SUPPORT WE'LL BLAME 'MICROSOFT.'"

It's common to write documentation for things that don't yet exist. As you might guess, it's frustrating.

I FEEL LIKE TWEAKING SOME BRITTLE PEOPLE. DO YOU KNOW ANY BRITTLE PEOPLE?

TRY TINA THE TECH WRITER. SHE BELIEVES THAT ALL FORMS OF EXPRESSION ARE AN INSULT TO HER GENDER AND HER PROFESSION.

THE STATUE OF "VENUS DE MILO" HAS NO ARMS.

OH, I GET IT. YOU'RE SAYING THAT WOMEN CAN'T LIFT HEAVY OBJECTS.

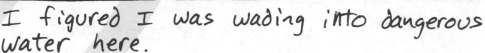

I figured I was wading into dangerous water here.

DOGBERT TWEAKS TINA THE BRITTLE TECH WRITER.

WHAT DO YOU THINK OF THE MOVIE "THELMA AND LOUISE"?

I KNOW WHAT YOU'RE TRYING TO SAY. YOU THINK ALL WOMEN ARE BAD DRIVERS. THAT'S REALLY THE POINT OF THE MOVIE, ISN'T IT??

IF YOU'RE NOT OFFENDED YET, TUNE IN TOMORROW.

THE "THREE STOOGES"?

WHY ARE ALL OF THE DOCUMENTARIES ABOUT MEN??!

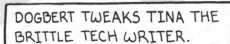

Controversy is good. That's my motto.

DOGBERT TWEAKS TINA THE BRITTLE TECH WRITER

IS TECHNICAL WRITING THE SAME AS WORD PROCESSING?

NO!!!

I AM A HIGHLY SKILLED COMMUNICATIONS PROFESSIONAL! I CAN TAKE JUMBLES OF INERT THOUGHTS AND BRING THEM TO LIFE!!

MY SECRETARY IS RUNNING THE STAFF MEETING. I NEED YOU TO RETYPE THIS ORG CHART.

THE DOCTOR IS IN!

8/31 © 1995 United Feature Syndicate, Inc.(NYC)

This is a pet peeve of Technical Writers.

THIS WEEK WE INTRODUCED TINA THE BRITTLE TECH WRITER TO THE STRIP. TINA IS DYSFUNCTIONAL LIKE EVERYBODY HERE EXCEPT ME.

RRRR

SEND YOUR OPINIONS BY E-MAIL TO SCOTTADAMS@AOL.COM

IT'S THE ONLY WAY WE CAN LEARN.

RRRR

9/1 © 1995 United Feature Syndicate, Inc.(NYC)

PICK ONE

A. WOMEN SHOULD ONLY BE PORTRAYED AS LAWYERS AND STARSHIP CAPTAINS.

B. I DON'T HAVE E-MAIL.

C. TINA SHOULD BE TREATED WITH THE SAME DIGNITY AS DILBERT AND WALLY.

D. TAKE AN ART CLASS.

Sadly, choice "D" was very popular.

A WHILE BACK I ASKED FOR OPINIONS ABOUT THIS NEW CHARACTER, "TINA THE BRITTLE TECH WRITER."

RRRR

RESULTS

MOST PEOPLE, INCLUDING NEARLY ALL SELF-DESCRIBED FEMINISTS, SAID KEEP HER. BUT THERE WERE MANY REQUESTS TO ADD "NON-STEREOTYPICAL" FEMALE CHARACTERS FOR BALANCE.

IN THE INTEREST OF BALANCE I GIVE YOU "ANTINA."

IS ANYBODY UP FOR SOME MATH?

1/1/96 © 1995 United Feature Syndicate, Inc. (NYC)

HI, I'M ANTINA THE NON-STEREOTYPICAL WOMAN.

THAT COMPUTER MONITOR YOU'RE USING IS SUPPOSED TO BE 17 INCHES. BUT IT'S MORE LIKE 16.5 INCHES.

I TOOK THE COFFEE MACHINE APART JUST FOR FUN — WANT TO SEE?

The hidden joke is that Dilbert's tie is flat by the third frame. I'm not sure what it means.

WALLY, I'M HOPING YOU'LL AGREE TO WRITE ABOUT YOUR PROJECT FOR THE NEWSLETTER...

AND IN THE GRAND TRADITION OF ENGINEERING, I EXPECT YOU'LL GIVE THIS THE LOWEST PRIORITY, THUS MAKING ME DESPISE YOU.

SO... ARE YOU SAYING YOU DON'T DESPISE ME NOW?

WE ARE NOT HAVING A "MOMENT" HERE!

Nobody complained that Wally was being a stereotypical male here.

PERFORMANCE REVIEW
YOUR MAIN ACCOMPLISHMENT WAS THE DEPARTMENT NEWSLETTER WHICH WAS BOTH UNINTERESTING AND UNIMPORTANT. YOU GET NO RAISE.

THE NEWSLETTER WAS YOUR IDEA, AND IT'S BORING BECAUSE MOST OF THE ARTICLES ARE CONTRIBUTED BY MY IDIOTIC COWORKERS.

YOU DON'T SEEM TO UNDERSTAND THE VALUE OF TEAMWORK.

I UNDERSTAND ITS VALUE; IT JUST COST ME A TWO-PERCENT RAISE.

This is another Technical Writer's pet peeve.

183

This was the first glimpse of the Elbonian culture.

I like the idea of an entire country of idiots.

Elbonians

Elbonians Elbonia is an underdeveloped country that comes in handy when I want to involve a foreign location in the strip without hurting my sales of **Dilbert** overseas. People think I have some specific country in mind when I write about Elbonia, but I don't. It represents the view that Americans have of any country that doesn't have cable television—we think they all wear fur hats and wallow around in waist-deep mud.

Some people think the Elbonians are surrounded by snow, but it's mud. I can't color the mud because the Elbonians have shaded clothing and I'd lose the contrast. It's one of those bothersome trade-offs that untalented cartoonists have to make. If you want to think of it as snow, that's okay too.

DILBERT TAKES ELBONIA AIRLINES. HE'S BEEN ASKED TO NEGOTIATE AN END TO THE ELBONIAN CIVIL WAR.

I CAN SUCCEED IF I FIND SOME WAY TO IMPRESS THE REBEL LEADER THEY CALL "THE FOX."

THE FOX IS DEAD!!

YOU CRUSHED OUR LEADER. NOW YOU MUST BE THE NEW REBEL LEADER.

I'M A DIPLOMAT, ON A PEACE MISSION.

A WISE ELBONIAN ONCE SAID "IN A RACE BETWEEN A ROCK AND A PIG, DON'T VARNISH YOUR CLAMS."

THAT'S STUPID.

WHAT KIND OF DIPLOMAT ARE YOU??

FIRST DAY ON THE JOB... GIMME A BREAK

Engineers would not be good diplomats.

WE LEFT-HANDED ELBONIANS HAVE BEEN PERSECUTED FOR CENTURIES. WE MUST CRUSH THE RIGHTIES!

DON'T YOU SEE THAT IT'S ONLY AN ARBITRARY DISTINCTION? ISN'T IT OBVIOUS THAT PEOPLE ARE THE SAME NO MATTER WHAT HAND THEY FAVOR?

NO, THAT ISN'T OBVIOUS TO US AT ALL.

GEEZ, YOU LEFTIES ARE THICK. I'M GLAD I'M NORMAL.

ELBONIANS HEAR ME! YOU MUST END YOUR FUTILE CIVIL WAR.

YOU'VE BEEN LOVING YOUR ANIMALS AND FIGHTING EACH OTHER. A CIVILIZED COUNTRY SHOULD SLAUGHTER THE ANIMALS AND SIMPLY DISCRIMINATE ECONOMIC-ALLY AGAINST EACH OTHER!

HOW DID MY SPEECH GO OVER?

I'M SOLD, BUT I THINK THE SECRETARY OF STATE WAS A BIT PUT OFF.

11-24

I'll take any excuse to draw animals.

IN A WAY, I'M GLAD THE ELBONIANS RUN THIS COMPANY NOW.

AFTER YEARS OF BEING THE ONLY FEMALE ENGIN-EER I'LL ENJOY WATCH-ING THE FIBONIANS DISCRIMINATE AGAINST YOU GUYS.

CONTINUED...

I DIDN'T REALIZE YOU HAD COFFEE WENCHES IN THIS COUNTRY TOO.

I HOPE YOU DON'T WANT CHILDREN, YORGI.

IN THIS COUNTRY WE HAVE A CUSTOM WHEN MEN ASK WOMEN TO FETCH COFFEE.

STAND UP... THAT'S IT... NOW THIS WILL REALLY SURPRISE YOU.

OH GOD

I'VE NEVER SEEN ANYBODY GET KICKED INTO HIS HAT BEFORE.

THAT'S GOTTA HURT.

I got complaints for using God's name in vain. I maintain it **187** is a prayer.

In 1989, the boss was tall, thin, and not so pointy-haired.

THE BOSS

The Pointy-Haired Boss (PHB) has no other name.
That's intentional. You can more easily imagine him to be your own boss if he has no name.

The original boss had jowls and nonpointy hair. He looked meaner and gruffer that way, but over time his looks and his personality evolved. Now he's more noncaring than he is overtly mean, and more clueless than gruff.

PHB's hair became pointier over time. It started as a gradual change that had no real purpose. One day I noticed it was getting pointier and I liked it. So I decided to go with it and push the hair toward full-blown, demonic horns. It fits his personality perfectly.

WELL, DILBERT, YOU SEEM QUALIFIED FOR THIS PROMOTION, BUT I HAVE ONE CONCERN. SINCE YOUR WORK WOULD BE EVALUATED BY MANY PEOPLE...

9-21   S.Adams

CAN YOU HANDLE CRITICISM?

OH, EASILY. FOR EXAMPLE, YOUR TOUPEE LOOKS LIKE A MULE-STOMPED GOPHER...

© 1989 United Feature Syndicate, Inc.

...TURNS OUT IT WAS A TRICK QUESTION.

BOY, YOU CAN'T TRUST THOSE BALD GUYS.

DILBERT

By Scott Adams

I have a sock monkey. They're great. You should get one.

He's not sadistic, just uncaring.

There was a time when all we talked about is how things were done in Japan. I think some of what they did was just pranks on us.

Jowls .... No Jowls .... Jowls

This became one of the most popular strips I've done.

Humor is relative.

Here he's still in his "cruel" phase.

194

It must be frustrating to be a boss and not have the option of hurting employees.

This is based closely on real life, except for the fighting.

This was another huge hit. Most employees have been in a meeting like that.

I like to have the characters do the things I would want to do in their position.

I got complaints from Temp agencies.

I wonder why this never caught on in the United States.

A huge frustration for technology workers is the imbecile boss.

"TIM WILL BE LEAVING THE COMPANY TO PURSUE OTHER OPPORTUNITIES."

NOTE THE ABSENCE OF KEY PHRASES SUCH AS "WE REGRET" OR "YEARS OF DEDICATED SERVICE." AND NOTICE THAT HIS NEW OPPORTUNITY IS NOT CALLED "EXCITING."

I THINK YOU'RE READING A LITTLE TOO MUCH INTO THAT ANNOUNCEMENT.

NO, I'M READING THE FOOTNOTE

I drew this left-handed because I was having hand problems. The lettering gives it away.

YOU'VE COMPLETELY ELIMINATED THE BUDGET FOR TECHNICAL TRAINING!

I'M GETTING DUMBER EVERY MINUTE. MY BRAIN IS STARTING TO SHRIVEL LIKE A RAISIN!

GET OUT OF MY OFFICE.

EVEN MY HAIR FEELS DIFFERENT.

The boss's hair has become a symbol for clueless management.

I CAN ASSURE YOU THAT THE VALUE OF THE AVERAGE EMPLOYEE WILL CONTINUE TO INCREASE.

IS THAT BECAUSE THERE WILL BE LESS OF US, DOING MORE WORK?

I'M RIGHT, AREN'T I?

EXCEPT FOR THE "US" PART.

Employees can get used to anything.

199

← This explains most levels of management.

This is the peak of pointiness, hair-wise.

I had a boss who tried this technique on me, with
similar success.

I hate this cartoon. 202 I was tired.

Do you remember when everyone was on the same side?

This strip was so popular that the phrase "Bungee Boss" has entered the vocabulary at some companies.

I waited in a lot of hallways at Pacific Bell.

I'm constantly hearing about employees getting in trouble for putting Dilbert cartoons on their cubicles.

Somewhere, you know someone has tried this.

DILBERT
BY
SCOTT ADAMS

BOSS TYPES

FIND YOUR BOSS ON THIS HANDY REFERENCE.

HOSTAGE TAKER: TRAPS YOU IN YOUR CUBICLE AND TALKS YOUR EARS OFF.

BLAH BLAH

OW!!

FRAUD: USES VIGOROUS HEAD-NODDING TO SIMULATE COMPREHENSION.

THEN WE'LL SUBNET OUR IP ADDRESSES.

OH YEAH OH YEAH

MOTIVATIONAL LIAR: HAS NO CLUE WHAT YOU DO BUT SAYS YOU'RE THE BEST.

NOBODY CAN DO WHAT YOU DO!!

EXCEPT A MUSHROOM.

OVER PROMOTED: TRIES TO MASK INCOMPETENCE WITH POOR COMMUNICATION.

LET'S QUALITIZE OUR PARADIGM SO WE DON'T OVER INUNDATE WITH DATUMS.

WEASEL: TAKES CREDIT FOR YOUR HARD WORK.

THIS BONUS IS FOR BRILLIANTLY FORCING YOUR STAFF TO WORK 80 HOUR WEEKS.

IT WASN'T EASY!

MOSES: PERPETUALLY WAITS FOR CLEAR SIGNALS FROM ABOVE.

DON'T DO ANYTHING IMPORTANT YET.

NEVER HAVE.

PERFECT BOSS: DIES OF NATURAL CAUSES ON A THURSDAY AFTERNOON.

SHOULD WE DO SOMETHING?

THREE DAY WEEKEND!

Do any of these look familiar?

This — by far — is the most popular cartoon I've ever drawn.

↖ That's based on reality.

A phrase you never want to hear is "hands-on manager."

So many people asked for a boss doll after this came out that we made one. **207**

This was the first appearance of Alice. She didn't have the distinct attitude she has now.

The "xerox" machine is a good place to reproduce.

I had a long discussion with my editor about this one.

ALICE

Alice wasn't always Alice. In the beginning there were a variety of fluffy-haired female characters in Dilbert's office but they didn't have many lines. Over time the personality of my friend and co-worker at Pacific Bell started to channel into the strip, emerging as the recurring character Alice. Alice's real-world counterpart (actual name Anita) was the model for Alice's pink suit, her fluffy hair, her long work hours, her coffee obsession, her technical proficiency, and her take-no-crap attitude.

As far as I know, the human version of Alice has never kicked a man into his hat, stuffed an intern into his shirt sleeve, or slapped a man so hard he traveled back in time. But if I ever hear about it happening, it won't surprise me.

Alice's hair has become bigger and more triangular for no real reason except that I like it that way. It's a challenge to keep it in the frame some-times but it's worth it.

This is a suggestion of the Alice to come.

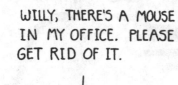 I stuck Dilbert here so you'd know what comic you were reading.

This was a generic Alice-like character.

This is a cheap laugh, but I'm not proud.

It's tough to be the only woman in engineering.

I CAN'T KEEP WORKING THESE LONG HOURS... I DESERVE A FAMILY LIFE.

ALICE, ALICE, ALICE...

THIS ISN'T THE "ME" GENERATION OF THE EIGHTIES. THIS IS THE "LIFELESS NINETIES." I EXPECT 178 HOURS OF WORK FROM YOU EACH WEEK.

10-20

THERE ARE ONLY... UH, 168 HOURS IN A WEEK.

I EXPECT YOUR FAMILY TO CHIP IN A FEW HOURS.

Alice's personality is becoming fully formed at this point.

I'M WORKING TOO MANY HOURS... I NEVER SPEND TIME WITH MY FAMILY.

THE COMPANY CARES. THAT'S WHY WE'VE DEVELOPED A PROGRAM TO TEACH YOU HOW TO COPE.

10-21

"CELIBACY AND ADOPTION — THE CHOICE FOR THE NINETIES."

DILBERT, I'M SENDING YOU TO "DIVERSITY SENSITIVITY" TRAINING.

ALICE DOESN'T HAVE TO GO BECAUSE CHICKS ARE BORN ALREADY KNOWING THIS STUFF. IT'S AS NATURAL AS SHOPPING AND CRYING.

5-31

CAN I GET A "MIDOL" FOR EITHER ONE OF YOU?

WHUMP WHUMP WHUMP

She's overworked, so she has a reason to be cranky.

I'M PROTESTING THE COMPANY'S DRESS CODE. I REFUSE TO DRESS LIKE A WOMAN.

HIGH HEELS AND PANTY-HOSE ARE DESIGNED TO MAKE WOMEN LOOK LIKE HELPLESS LITTLE ORNAMENTS FOR THE PLEASURE OF MALE VIEWERS!

I'VE NEVER HAD PLEASURE VIEWING YOU. I SWEAR.

THANK YOU FOR YOUR SUPPORT.

The hair has taken a vaguely pyramid shape.

I'M DRESSING LIKE A MAN TO PROTEST THE COMPANY'S DRESS CODE.

SO, WHAT YOU'RE SAYING IS THAT YOU'RE ACTUALLY A WOMAN. IS THAT YOUR CLAIM?

THAT'S NOT EXACTLY THE POINT.

I SAW "THE CRYING GAME." DON'T DO ANYTHING THAT WOULD MAKE ME HEAVE.

WHEN YOU CONSIDER THE HOURS I WORK, I MAKE LESS PER HOUR THAN THE JANITOR!

2/10

LOOK WHAT WAS BLOCKING THE PIPES! IT TOOK ME ALL MORNING TO PLUNGE THE RASCAL OUT.

I LOVE MY JOB.

I'M GIVING HIM A RAISE.

↶ I don't know what that is.

213

I've noticed that women care about their performance reviews far more than men do. (Yeah, I know it's an unfair generalization.)

This explains it.

No matter how good a performance review is, it's never good enough.

This tradition will live forever.

This is just a mouse, not Ratbert.

Wally is always trying to work the system.

This was inspired by a woody Allen movie where woody played a court jester. I liked the look.

There were a number of pre-**Wally** characters who had similar looks and bit parts in Dilbert's office. The true Wally didn't emerge until one of my co-workers at Pacific Bell found himself in an unusual situation: He wanted to leave the company, but not without getting one of the generous buyout packages that were being offered as part of the larger downsizing efforts. Unfortunately, the buyouts were limited to people who were identified as being in the lowest ten percent of the performers. That created a bizarre incentive for my co-worker to try as hard as he could to become the worst possible employee in order to get money for leaving. This wouldn't have been so fun to watch except that this fellow was one of the more brilliant people I've met and he was totally dedicated to this goal.

I loved the concept of a thoroughly cynical employee who has no sense of company loyalty and feels no need to mask his poor performance or his total lack of respect. Wally was born.

You can never be sure when Wally is being sarcastic.

Bad things happen to Wally. He takes it in stride.

Some women complained because they said I'm implying that being female is a punishment.

That's actually Wally, but it's not obvious.

I've noticed that other people can be inflexible.

DILBERT®

BY **SCOTT ADAMS**

WALLY, YOU NEVER REALLY ANSWERED THE QUESTION I LEFT ON YOUR VOICE-MAIL.

IS THIS A CASE OF SIMPLE INCOMPETENCE OR A PREVIEW OF SOMETHING FAR MORE SINISTER?

IT'S THE SINISTER ONE.

I'VE ADOPTED A DEFENSIVE STRATEGY. I'M WITHHOLDING INFORMATION TO MAKE MYSELF APPEAR MORE VALUABLE.

NOW I ONLY RETURN PHONE CALLS LATE AT NIGHT AND LEAVE INCOMPLETE ANSWERS.

IN PERSON, I ACT OVERWORKED AND IRRATIONAL SO PEOPLE STOP ASKING QUESTIONS.

IF CORNERED, I SIGH DEEPLY AND RECOUNT OLD WAR STORIES THAT DON'T RELATE TO THE QUESTION.

GOT IT!

NO CO-WORKER CAN THWART ME!

WHAT IF THEY TEAM UP?

© 1994 United Feature Syndicate, Inc.   1-1-95

S. Adams

There's always someone like this in every group.   221

I spent 17 years in corporate jobs and never did anything that made an impact. I don't think I was alone.

Wally is easy to draw, so he gets a lot of face time.

Wally has been married but now he's single.

Wally is the kind of guy who shouldn't have power.

. . . and Hygiene Issues

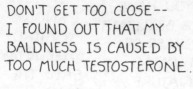

DON'T GET TOO CLOSE -- I FOUND OUT THAT MY BALDNESS IS CAUSED BY TOO MUCH TESTOSTERONE.

NOW WITH MY HAIR GONE I'M AFRAID THE TESTOSTERONE WILL START FLINGING OUT OF MY PORES.

4-12

HEY! YOU GOT SOME ON MY SHIRT!

DO YOU HAVE A PROBLEM WITH THAT?

I'm glad that baldness is becoming somewhat fashionable.

GEE, WALLY, YOU SURE HAVE BEEN POPULAR WITH WOMEN SINCE THE TESTOSTERONE STARTED SPEWING FROM YOUR HEAD.

4-14

IT'S AMAZING... I EVEN BOUGHT A PICKUP TRUCK AND A RIFLE SO I CAN HUNT AFTER WORK.

WHAT DO YOU HUNT AROUND HERE?

PIGEONS ARE THE MOST CONVENIENT... DON'T EVEN HAVE TO GET OUT OF THE TRUCK.

I GUESS IT'S TIME TO GO BACK TO MY DIMLY LIT CUBICLE AND SEE IF MY CARPAL TUNNEL HAS CRIPPLED ME YET.

7-16

THIS IS A LOT LIKE MY LAST JOB AS A COAL MINER, BUT WITHOUT THE THREAT OF A GAS EXPLOSION.

I'M MOVING YOU TO A NEW CUBICLE OVER BY WALLY.

BETTER GET A CANARY.

You see, miners use canaries to sense gas...

← My motto.

On the Internet, everyone is a bully.

"sponge bath" is a good comedy phrase.

225

I've had big problems with secretaries.

↑ This became a Dilbert book title.

CAROL

Carol Sometimes you'll find a secretary who likes and respects the boss and is helpful to everyone else in the office. But more often you get the "secretary from hell" who hates her job and finds perverse joy in making everyone within a two-mile radius suffer. Carol is one of the secretaries who tries to get as much of this sadistic joy as possible. She's a composite of all the bad experiences I've ever had with any secretary, and there have been many.

227

The "secretary with a crossbow" came from an e-mail message from a secretary who said she sometimes wished she had one.

THE "SECRETARY WITH A CROSSBOW" GOES ON THE HUNT.

MOBY DICK!

YOU'VE BEEN HARPOONED AGAIN, SIR.

YEAH, BUT I CAPSIZED HER DESK.

CAROL, THE NEXT TIME YOU ORDER MY BUSINESS CARDS, SPELL OUT MY FULL TITLE: "DIRECTOR OF PRODUCT ENHANCEMENTS."

DON'T USE THE ACRONYM "DOPE."

I DIDN'T KNOW YOU WERE THE DIRECTOR OF PRODUCT ENHANCEMENTS.

I hear lots of stories of initials that spell words.

HERE'S MY TIME SHEET, FILLED OUT IN INCREMENTS OF FIFTEEN MINUTES.

AS USUAL, I CODED THE USELESS HOURS SPENT IN MEETINGS AS "WORK," WHEREAS THE TIME I SPENT IN THE SHOWER DESIGNING CIRCUITS IN MY MIND IS "NON-WORK."

INTERESTINGLY, EVEN THE TIME I SPEND COMPLAINING ABOUT MY LACK OF PRODUCTIVITY IS CONSIDERED "WORK."

I HATE MY LIFE.

what exactly is "work" for a person who is paid to think?

WE'RE POISED FOR SUCCESS. WE EXPECT HUGE EARNINGS AND INCREASED MARKET SHARE!

NEXT ON THE AGENDA... THERE WILL BE NO RAISES BECAUSE IT WILL BE A DIFFICULT YEAR...

CAROL, I THOUGHT I TOLD YOU TO PUT THE "UNITED WAY" UPDATE BETWEEN THOSE TWO AGENDA ITEMS.

OOPSIE.

Carol's not-so-secret desire is to kill her evil boss.

CAROL, ABOUT THIS FLIGHT TO NEW YORK THAT YOU BOOKED FOR ME...

IS IT REALLY NECESSARY TO MAKE ALL THESE STOPOVERS IN THIRD-WORLD COUNTRIES THAT ARE EXPERIENCING REBEL INSURRECTIONS?

YOU'D BETTER WEAR THE INTERNATIONAL SYMBOL OF THE "RED CROSS" ON YOUR BACK.

YIKES !!!
A SKUNK IN
THE HOUSE !!!

HI.

OH, DON'T WORRY; WE SKUNKS ONLY SPRAY WHEN WE'RE SCARED... I CERTAINLY WOULDN'T USE MY THREATENING POWER TO FORCE YOU TO DO MY BIDDING.

THEN WHY IS YOUR TAIL TWITCHING ?!

I'M SCARED YOU MIGHT NOT OFFER ME A BIG BOWL OF STRAWBERRY ICE CREAM.

© 1989 United Feature Syndicate, Inc.

12-14

I used to work at a mountain resort where the skunks would walk through the kitchen without fear.

DILBERT IS THREATENED BY AN ABUSIVE SKUNK.

THAT'S RIGHT: A BIG BOWL OF ICE CREAM COULD KEEP ME FROM BEING AFRAID AND REFLEXIVELY SPRAYING YOUR LIVING ROOM.

THIS IS BLACKMAIL!

MY GOODNESS, NO. IT'S JUST THAT I CAN'T CONTROL MY FEAR RESPONSE.

© 1989 United Feature Syndicate, Inc.

NOW I'M AFRAID THAT YOU WON'T SING THE SONGS FROM "CATS" WHILE I EAT.

12-15

DILBERT, GO DOWN TO THE ACCOUNTING DEPARTMENT AND FIND OUT WHAT THESE FIGURES MEAN.

GULP

© 1990 United Feature Syndicate, Inc.

NO... P-PLEASE... THEY AREN'T EVEN HUMAN THERE !!!

8-13

I DON'T LIKE HIM.

SURPRISE.

Some of my worst business experiences involve accounting.

CRITTERS

Miscellaneous Critters Some people remind me of particular animals. I love to substitute the actual animal for human beings in the strip because it sends such a clear message. Everyone understands what I mean when I represent the accounting department as trolls or the marketing guy as a weasel. When Dilbert's blind date turns out to be a literal dog it seems oddly familiar.

Here are some of my favorite strips that feature animals and other strange creatures.

FOOL! WHY HAVE YOU COME TO THE ACCOUNTING DEPARTMENT?!!

S.Adams

© 1990 United Feature Syndicate, Inc.

UH... I HAD SOME QUESTIONS, SIR... MA'AM ... ER, SIR?

ARE YOU A MAN OR WOMAN?

IN ACCOUNTING, IT DOESN'T REALLY MATTER.

8-15

Do any accountants in big companies have good attitudes?

← People who work with numbers start to believe this.

Turtles seem like the dumbest pets to have. Even the "Pet Rock" had funny instructions.

You see, turtles are slow...

This is just like my dinosaur egg joke you saw earlier.

DILBERT, YOUR NEW CO-WORKER IS ZIMBU THE MONKEY.

ZIMBU LEARNED ENGLISH FROM THE ZOO KEEPERS IN A SPECIAL PROGRAM.

THIS MONKEY IS AN INSULT TO THE INTELLIGENCE OF THE OTHER WORKERS AND I!

OTHER WORKERS AND "ME," NOT "I"!

Much of my cubicle jobs could have been done by monkeys.

PRAIRIE DOGS

OFFICE WORKERS

PRAIRIE DOG WORKERS

MAN, I'M SWAMPED.

whenever there was a loud noise, the cubicles looked like prairie dog habitats.

I ALWAYS THOUGHT YOU BEAVERS WERE BUSY ALL THE TIME.

THAT'S A COMMON STEREOTYPE. I'M ACTUALLY QUITE LAZY.

HOW DO YOU BUILD YOUR BEAVER HOME?

I RENT.

I love the concept of a lazy beaver. But he doesn't fit into the strip.

234

I think it's the coffee cup that sells this character.

I made up the name Zimbu because it sounds like a monkey name to me.

Why don't people have tails?

I wish I had a tail.

Some day we'll look back and be amazed that we put up with cubicles.

This used to be my job, but I was less ethical.

OUR CEO CANCELLED HIS VISIT. HE'S SENDING HIS TOP AID, ZIMBU THE MONKEY, IN HIS PLACE.

ISN'T THAT TYPICAL? I SPENT A WEEK EXAGGERATING MY ACCOMPLISHMENTS FOR THIS. NOW HE SENDS A STUPID MONKEY!

WHAT COULD BE MORE HUMILIATING THAN TRYING TO SUCK-UP TO A MONKEY?

FAILING AT IT?

The harder you prepare, the less likely the meeting will happen.

HA HA! NOW THAT THE ENGINEERS MUST CHARGE THEIR TIME TO MARKETING, WE OWN YOU!

I'LL JUST REPROGRAM YOUR COMPUTER THROUGH THE LAN SO ITS RADIATION WILL ALTER YOUR DNA.

IS THAT POSSIBLE??!

AS FAR AS YOU KNOW.

This is the only defense the engineers have.

I TOLD A GUY IN MARKETING THAT I PROGRAMMED HIS COMPUTER TO ALTER HIS DNA STRUCTURE.

HEE HEE

HE THINKS HE'LL TURN INTO SOME KIND OF ANIMAL.

TELL HIM YOU SET IT TO "WEASEL." IT'LL TAKE LONGER TO NOTICE ANY CHANGE.

TELL ME THE TRUTH, ALICE. CAN DILBERT REPROGRAM MY DNA?

YEAH. YOU MARKETING GUYS ONLY HAVE ONE HELIX.

People would be much cuter if we all had round noses and big whiskers.

I've had this feeling.

THE DEHUMANIZATION OF MY JOB HAS RENDERED ME INVISIBLE TO HUMANS. ONLY YOU CAN SEE ME, DOGBERT.

HOW CAN WE FIX THIS?

YOU COULD WEAR A BAG ON YOUR HEAD WHEN YOU'RE AROUND ME.

THAT'S NOT THE FIX I HAD IN MIND.

IT'S NOT A PERFECT SOLUTION. I'D STILL BE ABLE TO HEAR YOU.

The only cure for workplace invisibility is to screw something up.

YOU'RE INVISIBLE TO YOUR CO-WORKERS. BUT YOU CAN COMPENSATE BY FORMING A SYMBIOTIC RELATIONSHIP WITH A VISIBLE CREATURE.

RATBERT WILL CLING TO YOUR BACK. HE'LL BE YOUR VISUAL AND AUDITORY LINK WITH YOUR CO-WORKERS.

SO... WORKING HARD? OR HARDLY WORKING?

I KNEW THIS COLOMBIAN COFFEE WAS TROUBLE.

I got a complaint from a Colombian who didn't like the coffee reference.

DON'T BE ALARMED. I'M NOT REALLY A RAT FLOATING IN MIDAIR.

I'M CLINGING TO THE BACK OF AN EMPLOYEE WHO HAS BEEN RENDERED INVISIBLE BY A LONG SUCCESSION OF WORTHLESS ASSIGNMENTS.

LOOKS LIKE AN ISOLATED CASE OF BAD ATTITUDE.

WHICH ROOM IS THE "QUALITY" MEETING IN?

I'm always shy in restaurants.

DOGBERT

Dogbert in Hats There are few things in life that are as funny as a dog in a hat. Since Dogbert doesn't have many facial cues—no visible mouth or eyes—I can convey a lot about what he's thinking by giving him a funny hat.

I'VE DECIDED TO BECOME A POP PSYCHOLOGIST. I NEED YOUR HELP TO MAKE MY LECTURE VIDEO.

YOU CAME TO THE RIGHT PLACE, BABE. FIRST, YOU NEED A NEW LOOK.

NICE TRY, BUT FRANKLY, THIS LOOK DIDN'T WORK TOO WELL FOR MADONNA EITHER.

7-30

© 1991 United Feature Syndicate, Inc.

NOSTRADOGBERT PREDICTS THERE WILL BE TURMOIL IN THE MIDDLE EAST.

12-11

WOW! THAT'S QUITE A PREDICTION! YOU'RE REALLY GOING OUT ON A LIMB!

© 1991 United Feature Syndicate, Inc.

IS THAT SARCASM? I CAN'T TELL WITH YOU.

WILL THERE BE ANY SAND INVOLVED?

The top of Dogbert's head is hard to draw. So I like hiding it with hats. **241**

WHAT DID YOU DO TO YOUR HAIR?

IT'S FOR MY NEW TELEVISION SHOW, "HEALING FOR DOLLARS." PEOPLE SEND MORE MONEY IF YOU HAVE THIS KIND OF HAIR.

6-15

It's true!

IT MIGHT BE A TRICK.

THAT'S WHAT I THOUGHT UNTIL I SAW HIS HAIR.

CHECKS OR MONEY ORDERS

WHY SHOULD I OPEN IT? YOU ALREADY TOLD ME IT'S JUST A STUPID HAT.

OPEN IT ANYWAY.

12-25

HEY, IT'S NOT REALLY A HAT; IT'S A CROWN.

I'M NOT HAPPY. I'M ONLY HUMORING YOU.

MERRY CHRISTMAS, LITTLE FRIEND.

I DECLARE MYSELF THE PATRON SAINT OF TECHNOLOGY.

1-31

I HEAL BROKEN TECHNOLOGY WITH MY RIGHT PAW AND I USE THE SCEPTER TO DRIVE OUT THE DEMONS OF STUPIDITY.

I DON'T THINK I'VE SEEN YOUR SPIRITUAL SIDE BEFORE.

OUT! OUT!

This hat design comes from a fancy folded napkin.

How many times have you heard that one?

This was based on a co-worker whose wife made his business suits.

The little dot-shading in Ted's hair is a pain, so now I just ink it black.

This is the most common "generic guy" I draw.

Ted the Generic Guy

Maybe you've noticed, but I don't have a wide artistic range. So when I need a new character to play a bit part, it often ends up looking like the same guy. Privately I call him "Ted, the generic guy," even though he sometimes has other aliases in the cartoon. Here are the many faces of Ted.

Ted started to be a regular but the other characters were more interesting.

DILBERT

By Scott Adams

DILBERT, I'D LIKE YOU TO INTRODUCE THE NEW GUY TO EVERYBODY.

GROAN

THIS WAY I NEVER HAVE TO LEARN THEIR NAMES.

THE FIRST STOP ON OUR ODYSSEY IS BUD.

UH... BUD, THIS IS THE NEW GUY, AND VICE-VERSA.

WHAT'S THIS?! ANOTHER PINK-BOTTOMED, IVY LEAGUE, MANAGEMENT "TRAINEE"?!

NEWS

IN MY DAY, YOU HAD TO START AT THE BOTTOM... AND BY GOLLY, YOU STAYED THERE!!

HOW LONG HAVE YOU WORKED HERE?

5-19

A WEEK... THIS HAPPENS PRETTY QUICKLY.

© 1991 United Feature Syndicate, Inc.

I met a "Bud" on my first day of work.

246

could we all just agree that babies are ugly and leave it at that?

If I have to fire or kill someone, it's often the generic guy.

LOOK, TED! WE GET PAID THE SAME AS YOU BUT ALL WE'RE DOING IS STANDING AROUND AND FLICKING OUR FINGERS.

COME JOIN US AND FLICK YOUR FINGERS IN JOYOUS CELEBRATION THAT OUR PERFORMANCE IS NOT LINKED TO OUR PAY.

FLICK FLICK

I DON'T KNOW WHAT SUCCESS SOUNDS LIKE, BUT I'LL BET THIS ISN'T IT.

FLICK FLICK FLICK FLICK FLICK

← often he gets no lines.

I DON'T KNOW WHAT KIND OF GIFT TO BUY FOR TED'S BABY SHOWER.

HAND-CRAFTED ITEMS ARE GOOD. CUT THREE HOLES IN A PAPER BAG AND YOU'VE GOT A LOVELY BABY DRESS.

HE MIGHT THINK I'M CHEAP.

DO YOU THINK THE KID HAS A SALT SHAKER YET?

TED'S BABY SHOWER

OH LOOK, IT'S A STAPLER...

I CAN USE THIS TO TAKE UP THE HEM ON THE LOVELY HAND-CRAFTED PAPER BAG DRESS THAT DILBERT MADE.

IT LOOKS JUST LIKE THE ONE THAT DISAPPEARED FROM MY CUBICLE THIS MORNING.

EXCEPT YOURS HAD STAPLES.

sometimes Ted has dot eyes instead of ʊ͜ʊ eyes.

It's not good to think about these things.

Only jelly donuts make the "sploit" noise.

Slapstick Strips

Slapstick Strips One of the advantages of comics is that people who deserve a slap or a wedgie can get one. But it has to be carefully done to avoid complaints. For example, it's funny when a dog smacks a person, but I could never get away with having a person smack a dog—that would be cruel.

Here's a selection of my favorite slapstick strips, proving once again that violence can be funny.

I think you could get people hooked on exploding cigars if you marketed them well.

DILBERT

By Scott Adams

Dilbert got tarred and feathered, in case it's hard to tell.

wouldn't this be fun?

Morale is a two-way street.

Don't send your vote. He was spared.

I was in a bad mood when I drew this.

It sounds naughty, but it isn't.

Dog hits man is funny, but not the other way around.